chicken
favourites

Your Promise of Success

Welcome to the world of Confident Cooking, created for you in our test kitchen, where recipes are double-tested by our team of home economists to achieve a high standard of success.

PERIPLUS

chicken stock

Home-made stock has a much better flavour than bought granules, cubes or tetra packs. This stock can be used as a soup base, for delicate sauces, and for poaching. Many of the recipes in the book require stock. So much the better if you use this home-made version, but the ready-made varieties are fine if you don't have the time to make your own.

1.5–1.8 kg (3 lb 5 oz–4 lb) chicken
1 onion, roughly chopped
1 leek, roughly chopped
1 carrot, roughly chopped
1 celery stalk, roughly chopped
2 bay leaves
6 black peppercorns
1 large thyme sprig

Makes 3.25 litres (13 cups)

1 Wash the chicken inside and out, then place it in a large saucepan or stockpot with the remaining ingredients. Pour in 3.5 litres (14 cups) cold water and slowly bring to the boil.

2 Skim off any scum that rises to the surface, using a skimmer or slotted spoon. As soon as the stock comes to the boil, reduce the heat and let it simmer very gently for 1½ hours. Don't boil the stock or it will turn cloudy.

3 Leave the stock to cool slightly before you strain it through a large colander to separate the chicken and vegetables from the liquid. Next, strain the liquid through a fine sieve to remove any bone, vegetable and herb fragments. The chicken can be eaten while still warm, or cooled completely, then refrigerated for later.

4 Allow the stock to cool completely before refrigerating it overnight. The next day, spoon off the layer of fat that has formed on top, and the stock is ready to use.

notes: Serve the warm chicken meat with some hollandaise or pesto for a delicious lunch, or refrigerate it to use later in pasta dishes, sandwiches and salads.

Stock will keep in the refrigerator for 3–4 days, or can be frozen for up to a month. Freeze it in plastic containers in usable quantities of 250 ml (1 cup) or 500 ml (2 cups).

chicken and vegetable soup

PREP TIME: 15 MINUTES
COOKING TIME: 40 MINUTES
SERVES 4-6

3.25 litres (13 cups) chicken stock from page 2 (reserve the chicken flesh)
1 large potato, cut into 2 cm (3/4 inch) cubes
2 carrots, sliced into rounds
1 large leek, sliced
100 g (3 1/2 oz) shelled peas
100 g (3 1/2 oz) green beans, trimmed and cut into 2 cm (3/4 inch) lengths
small pinch of cayenne pepper, optional
3 tablespoons chopped parsley

NUTRITION PER SERVE (6): Fat 10.5 g; Carbohydrate 12 g; Protein 36 g; Dietary Fibre 3.5 g; Cholesterol 141 mg; 1190 kJ (285 Cal)

1 Spoon away the layer of fat from the surface of the stock, then bring the stock to the boil in a large saucepan. Reduce the heat, then add the potato, carrot and leek to the stock and simmer for 10 minutes, or until the vegetables have softened. Add the peas and green beans, then simmer for another 15 minutes.

2 Pull the skin off the chicken, then tear the flesh from the bones and cut it into bite-sized chunks. Add the chicken to the soup, along with the cayenne pepper, and season well with salt and freshly ground black pepper. Simmer the soup for 10 minutes, or until the chicken is warmed through. Stir in the parsley just before serving.

chicken noodle soup

PREP TIME: 20 MINUTES
COOKING TIME: 25 MINUTES
SERVES 4-6

2 litres (8 cups) chicken stock
175 g (1 cup) finely shredded cooked chicken
100 g (1 cup) broken thin noodles
45 g (3/4 cup) chopped fresh parsley

NUTRITION PER SERVE (6): Fat 5 g; Carbohydrate 14 g; Protein 12.5 g; Dietary Fibre 1 g; Cholesterol 30 mg; 625 kJ (150 Cal)

1 Bring the stock to the boil in a large saucepan.

2 Reduce the heat, add the shredded chicken and simmer until the meat is warmed through. Stir in the noodles and simmer for 10–15 minutes or until tender. Stir in the chopped parsley just before serving.

notes: Noodles must be added close to serving time, otherwise they will soften too much on standing.

pictured: chicken and vegetable soup

cream of chicken soup

PREP TIME: 20 MINUTES
COOKING TIME: 1 HOUR
SERVES 4

100 g (3 1/2 oz) butter
1 onion, finely diced
2 garlic cloves, crushed
1 leek, white part only, finely chopped
2 celery stalks, finely chopped
200 g (7 oz) chicken breast, cut into 1 cm (1/2 inch) dice
3 tablespoons plain (all-purpose) flour
1 litre (4 cups) chicken stock
125 ml (1/2 cup) cream, plus 2 tablespoons, to serve
2 teaspoons finely chopped chives, to serve

NUTRITION PER SERVE: Fat 42 g; Carbohydrate 11.5 g; Protein 16 g; Dietary Fibre 2 g; Cholesterol 152.5 mg; 2010 kJ (480 Cal)

1 Melt the butter in a heavy-based saucepan over low heat, then add the onion, garlic, leek and celery. Sauté, stirring frequently so the vegetables don't brown, for 15 minutes (slowly sautéeing the vegetables at this stage allows their flavours to develop).

2 Add the chicken to the pan and cook, stirring occasionally, for 5 minutes. Add the flour and stir to combine thoroughly over the heat. Cook for 5 minutes, then slowly add the chicken stock, a little at a time, stirring well so that lumps don't form.

3 Bring to simmering point, then cook, uncovered, for 30 minutes. Allow to cool slightly before blending in batches until quite smooth. It is important to allow the soup to cool before putting it in the blender, as the pressure when the soup is hot may cause the blender lid to come loose and allow the soup to splatter. Pour the soup back into a clean saucepan, add the cream, then bring back to a simmer and season to taste.

4 Pour into serving bowls, swirl about 2 teaspoons of the extra cream through the middle of each bowl of soup, then scatter with chopped chives.

chicken and corn soup

PREP TIME: 20 MINUTES +
  10 MINUTES STANDING
COOKING TIME: 25 MINUTES
SERVES 4

750 ml (3 cups) chicken stock
2 chicken breast fillets
3–4 corn cobs
1 tablespoon oil
4 spring onions (scallions), thinly sliced, greens chopped and reserved for garnish
1 garlic clove, crushed
2 teaspoons grated fresh ginger
310 g (10 1/2 oz) tin creamed corn
1 tablespoon Chinese rice wine or dry sherry
2 tablespoons soy sauce
1 tablespoon cornflour (cornstarch)
2 teaspoons sesame oil

NUTRITION PER SERVE: Fat 14.5 g; Carbohydrate 34 g; Protein 30 g; Dietary Fibre 7.5 g; Cholesterol 66 mg; 1640 kJ (390 Cal)

1 Place the stock in a saucepan and bring to the boil. Add the chicken, cover and remove the pan from the heat. Allow the chicken to cool in the liquid. Remove the chicken with a slotted spoon, then finely shred the meat using your fingers.

2 Cut the corn kernels from the cobs to yield about 400 g (2 cups). Heat the oil in a heavy-based saucepan or wok and add the spring onion, garlic and ginger. Stir for 30 seconds, then add the stock, corn kernels, creamed corn, rice wine and soy sauce. Stir until the soup comes to the boil, then reduce the heat and simmer for about 10 minutes. Add the chicken meat.

3 Stir the cornflour, sesame oil and 1 tablespoon water together in a small bowl until smooth. Add a little of the hot stock, stir to blend, then pour this mixture into the soup. Bring to simmering point, stirring constantly for 3–4 minutes, or until slightly thickened. Taste and, if necessary, adjust the seasoning. Garnish with the chopped reserved spring onion.

vietnamese poached chicken salad

PREP TIME: 20 MINUTES +
  10 MINUTES STANDING
COOKING TIME: 10 MINUTES
SERVES 4–6

375 ml (1 1/2 cups) chicken stock
2 chicken breasts
2 red chillies, seeded and finely chopped
2 tablespoons grated palm sugar or soft brown sugar
2 garlic cloves, finely chopped
1 tablespoon rice vinegar (see Note)
3 tablespoons lime juice
3 tablespoons fish sauce
1 1/2 tablespoons oil
280 g (4 cups) shredded Chinese cabbage (see Note)
100 g (1 cup) grated carrot
10 g (1/2 cup) mint
2 tablespoons fried shallots plus extra, to garnish
coriander (cilantro) sprigs, to garnish
lime wedges, to serve
prawn (shrimp) crackers, to serve

NUTRITION PER SERVE (6): Fat 8 g; Carbohydrate 6.5 g; Protein 16 g; Dietary Fibre 1.5 g; Cholesterol 44 mg; 675 kJ (160 Cal)

1 Pour the stock into a saucepan and bring to the boil. Remove from the heat, add the chicken to the stock, then cover and allow to cool in the liquid. After about 10 minutes, the chicken should be cooked. Test by touching with your finger—the chicken should feel quite springy.

2 To make the dressing, put the chilli, palm sugar, garlic, rice vinegar, lime juice, fish sauce and oil in a bowl and stir together.

3 Shred the chicken meat and place in a bowl with the shredded Chinese cabbage, carrot, mint and fried shallots. Add the dressing and place well. Garnish with fresh coriander sprigs and some more fried shallots. Serve immediately with lime wedges and prawn crackers.

notes: Rice vinegar is made from vinegar and a natural rice extract. It is used in dressings and marinades. Chinese cabbage is also known as wom bok or napa cabbage. It has a mild, sweet flavour. It is smaller than normal cabbage, and is shaped like a cos lettuce with tightly packed leaves. If it's not available, use another curly-leaf cabbage instead.

chicken waldorf salad

PREP TIME: 15 MINUTES +
 10 MINUTES STANDING
COOKING TIME: 10 MINUTES
SERVES 4

375 ml (1 1/2 cups) chicken stock
2 chicken breasts
2 red apples, cut into bite-sized pieces
2 green apples, cut into bite-sized pieces
2 celery stalks, diced
100 g (1 cup) walnuts, toasted
125 g (1/2 cup) whole-egg mayonnaise
3 tablespoons sour cream
1/2 teaspoon chopped tarragon (optional)
baby cos leaves, to serve

NUTRITION PER SERVE: Fat 54 g; Carbohydrate 19.5 g; Protein 26.5 g; Dietary Fibre 4.5 g; Cholesterol 123 mg; 2755 kJ (660 Cal)

1 Pour the stock into a saucepan and bring to the boil. Remove from the heat, add the chicken to the stock, then cover and allow to cool in the liquid. After about 10 minutes, the chicken should be cooked. Test by touching with your finger—the chicken should feel quite springy.

2 Combine the chicken, apple, celery and walnuts in a bowl.

3 Mix together the mayonnaise, sour cream and tarragon and season lightly. Drizzle over the salad and serve with baby cos leaves.

chicken, mango and walnut salad

PREP TIME: 20 MINUTES
COOKING TIME: NIL
SERVES 4

3 smoked chicken breast fillets
4 celery stalks
2 mignonette lettuces, torn
2 large firm mangoes
50 g (1/2 cup) walnut halves
5 spring onions (scallions), thinly sliced
3 tablespoons mayonnaise
1 tablespoon lime juice
1 teaspoon Dijon mustard
3 tablespoons olive oil

NUTRITION PER SERVE: Fat 30 g; Carbohydrate 5.5 g; Protein 25 g; Dietary Fibre 5 g; Cholesterol 45 mg; 1585 kJ (380 cal)

1 Cut the chicken into bite-sized pieces and diagonally slice the celery. Arrange the lettuce on serving plates and top with the chicken and celery.

2 Slice the mangoes into bite-sized pieces, then add to the plates with the walnuts and half the spring onion.

3 Mix together the mayonnaise, lime juice, mustard and oil and drizzle over the salad. Serve sprinkled with the extra spring onion.

pictured: chicken waldorf salad

teriyaki chicken with ginger chive rice

PREP TIME: 10 MINUTES +
1 HOUR MARINATING
COOKING TIME: 20 MINUTES
SERVES 4

4 small chicken breast fillets, skin on
3 tablespoons Japanese soy sauce
2 tablespoons sake (see Notes)
1 1/2 tablespoons mirin (see Notes)
1 1/2 tablespoons soft brown sugar
3 teaspoons finely grated fresh ginger
300 g (1 1/2 cups) long-grain rice
2 tablespoons finely chopped chives
2 tablespoons oil

NUTRITION PER SERVE: Fat 27 g; Carbohydrate 66 g; Protein 39.5 g; Dietary Fibre 0.5 g; Cholesterol 124 mg; 2845 kJ (680 Cal)

1 Pound each breast between two sheets of plastic wrap with a mallet or rolling pin until 1 cm (1/2 in) thick.

2 Place the soy sauce, sake, mirin, sugar and 1 teaspoon of the ginger in a flat non-metallic dish big enough to fit all the chicken in a single layer and stir until the sugar has dissolved. Add the chicken and turn to coat. Cover and refrigerate for 1 hour, turning once halfway through.

3 Once the chicken has marinated, bring a saucepan of water to the boil. Add the rice and cook for 12 minutes, stirring occasionally. Drain. Stir in the chives and the remaining ginger, then cover until ready to serve.

4 Meanwhile, drain the chicken, reserving the marinade. Heat the oil in a large deep frying pan and cook the chicken, skin-side-down over medium heat for 4–5 minutes, or until the skin is crisp. Turn and cook the other side for 4 minutes—remove from the pan (the chicken should not be quite cooked through).

5 Add the reserved marinade and 3 tablespoons water to the pan and scrape any sediment stuck to the base. Bring to the boil over high heat, then return the chicken (skin-side-up) with any juices to the pan. Cook for 5–6 minutes, or until just cooked through, turning once to coat. (If the sauce is still a little runny, remove the chicken and boil the sauce over high heat until it is slightly syrupy.) Rest the chicken for a few minutes.

6 To serve, divide the rice among four serving plates and place the chicken (either whole or sliced on the diagonal) on top. Drizzle with a little sauce and serve with steamed Asian greens.

notes: Sake is an alcoholic liquid made by fermenting cooked, ground rice mash. It has a dry, sherry-like taste. Mirin is a sweet spirit-based rice liquid commonly used in Japanese cookery. These ingredients are available in Asian supermarkets, Japanese speciality stores and some large supermarkets in the Asian section.

steamed chicken with ginger and spring onion sauce

PREP TIME: 15 MINUTES
COOKING TIME: 20 MINUTES
SERVES 4

500 ml (2 cups) chicken stock
3 x 2 cm (1 1/4 x 3/4 inch) piece of fresh ginger, thinly sliced
1 garlic clove, thinly sliced
4 chicken breast fillets, skin removed, trimmed
2 tablespoons thinly sliced (on the diagonal) spring onion (scallion)
2 teaspoons finely julienned fresh ginger, extra
2 tablespoons soy sauce
2 tablespoons peanut oil
1/2 teaspoon sesame oil

NUTRITION PER SERVE: Fat 20.5 g; Carbohydrate 1.5 g; Protein 45 g; Dietary Fibre 0.5 g; Cholesterol 132 mg; 1555 kJ (370 Cal)

1 Pour the stock into a wok. Add the ginger and garlic, bring to the boil, then reduce the heat to low. Simmer gently for 5 minutes to allow the flavours to infuse.

2 Lightly season the chicken breasts with salt and freshly ground black pepper. Line a bamboo steamer basket with baking paper and place the chicken breasts on the paper, making sure the breasts aren't touching one another. Depending on the size of your steamer basket, you may need two steamer trays, or you may need to cook the breasts in two batches. If you don't have a wok and bamboo steamers, you can use a saucepan and place a metal steamer tray over it.

3 Cover the steamer and place it over the wok for 10 minutes, or until the breasts are cooked through. To test, touch the chicken to see if it is springy. Remove from the steamer, transfer to a plate and cover with foil for 3 minutes (leaving the chicken to rest allows the flesh to relax, resulting in tender and moist chicken). Slice the breast across the grain.

4 Scatter the spring onion and extra ginger over the chicken breasts. Pour the soy sauce over them. In a small pan, heat the peanut oil and sesame oil until hot, but not smoking. Carefully spoon the oil over the chicken and serve immediately.

tandoori chicken

PREP TIME: 15 MINUTES +
  OVERNIGHT MARINATING
COOKING TIME: 20 MINUTES
SERVES 6

- 1/2 teaspoon sweet smoked paprika
- 1 teaspoon paprika
- 1/2 teaspoon ground cumin
- 1/2 teaspoon ground coriander
- 1/4 teaspoon ground ginger
- 1/4 teaspoon ground cinnamon
- 1/4 teaspoon ground fenugreek seeds
- 1/4 teaspoon ground black pepper
- 1/4 teaspoon chilli powder
- 1/4 teaspoon ground cardamom
- 1/4 teaspoon ground caraway seeds
- 2 garlic cloves, crushed
- 2 tablespoons lemon juice
- 4 tablespoons finely chopped coriander (cilantro)
- 250 g (1 cup) Greek-style or other plain yoghurt
- 6 boneless chicken breasts
- 25 g (1 oz) ghee (see Note)

NUTRITION PER SERVE: Fat 17 g; Carbohydrate 4.5 g; Protein 45.5 g; Dietary Fibre 1.5 g; Cholesterol 153 mg; 1495 kJ (355 Cal)

1 Prepare the tandoori spice blend by mixing the sweet smoked paprika, paprika, cumin, coriander, ginger, cinnamon, fenugreek, black pepper, chilli powder, cardamom and caraway in a large ceramic or glass bowl or dish. Ceramic and glass are ideal for marinating because metal reacts with acids, such as lemon juice, and plastic absorbs strong flavours.

2 Add the crushed garlic, lemon juice, fresh coriander and yoghurt to the bowl and stir the mixture together. Add the chicken breasts and coat thoroughly with the marinade. Cover and refrigerate for at least 8 hours, or overnight.

3 Remove the chicken from the marinade and lightly season each side with salt. Heat a chargrill pan or heavy-based frying pan. Add the ghee and when it is hot, but not smoking, add the chicken and cook over low heat for 8–10 minutes each side, or until cooked through. Serve with steamed rice.

note: Ghee, a form of clarified butter, is used here because it has a higher smoke point than normal butter, which means it burns less readily.

satay chicken

PREP TIME: 30 MINUTES +
1 HOUR MARINATING
COOKING TIME: 30 MINUTES
SERVES 4-6

500 g (1 lb) chicken thigh fillets,
cut into 1 cm (1/2 inch) wide strips
1 garlic clove, crushed
2 teaspoons finely grated fresh ginger
3 teaspoons fish sauce

Satay sauce

2 teaspoons peanut oil
4 red Asian shallots, finely chopped
4 garlic cloves, crushed
2 teaspoons finely chopped fresh ginger
2 bird's eye chillies, seeded and finely
chopped
125 g (1/2 cup) crunchy peanut butter
250 ml (1 cup) coconut milk
2 teaspoons soy sauce
2 tablespoons grated palm sugar or soft
brown sugar (see Note)
1 1/2 tablespoons fish sauce
1 makrut (kaffir) lime leaf
1 1/2 tablespoons lime juice

NUTRITION PER SERVE (6): Fat 27 g; Carbohydrate 9 g;
Protein 24 g; Dietary Fibre 4 g; Cholesterol 72.5 mg;
1565 kJ (375 Cal)

1 Put the chicken, garlic, ginger and fish sauce in a non-metallic bowl and move the chicken around to coat well. Cover and refrigerate for 1 hour. Soak 12 wooden skewers in cold water for 30 minutes to prevent them burning during cooking.

2 Meanwhile, to make the satay sauce, heat the oil in a saucepan over medium heat, then add the shallots, garlic, ginger and chilli. Stir constantly with a wooden spoon for 5 minutes, or until the shallots are golden. Reduce the heat to low and add the remaining sauce ingredients. Simmer for 10–15 minutes, or until thickened. Remove from the heat and keep warm. Discard the lime leaf.

3 Thread 2–3 chicken strips onto each skewer. Don't crowd the skewers or the chicken won't cook evenly. Cook the chicken on a heated barbecue hot plate or chargrill pan, turning the skewers after 5 minutes. Cook for another 5 minutes, or until they are cooked through. Serve with the sauce.

note: Palm sugar is a rich, aromatic sugar made by tapping and boiling the juice of the sugar palm. It is available in blocks or jars from Asian grocers and large supermarkets.

lime and coriander chargrilled chicken

PREP TIME: 15 MINUTES +
 1 HOUR MARINATING
COOKING TIME: 15 MINUTES
SERVES 4

3 teaspoons finely grated fresh ginger
25 g (1/2 cup) chopped coriander (cilantro) leaves
1 1/4 teaspoons grated lime zest
4 tablespoons lime juice
4 skinless chicken breast fillets, trimmed
250 g (1 1/4 cups) jasmine rice
2 tablespoons oil
3 zucchini (courgettes), cut into wedges
4 large flat mushrooms, stalks trimmed

NUTRITION PER SERVE: Fat 20.5 g; Carbohydrate 52 g; Protein 47 g; Dietary Fibre 3 g; Cholesterol 123.5 mg; 2435 kJ (580 Cal)

1 Combine the ginger, coriander, lime zest and 2 tablespoons of the lime juice. Spread 2 teaspoons of the herb mixture over each fillet and season well. Marinate for 1 hour. Combine the remaining herb mixture with the remaining lime juice in a screwtop jar. Set aside until needed.

2 Bring a large saucepan of water to the boil. Add the rice and cook for 12 minutes. Drain well.

3 Meanwhile, heat a chargrill pan or barbecue hot plate to medium and lightly brush with oil. Brush the zucchini and mushrooms with the remaining oil. Place the chicken on the chargrill and cook on each side for 4–5 minutes, or until cooked through. Add the vegetables during the last 5 minutes of cooking, and turn frequently until browned on the outside and just softened. Cover with foil until ready to serve.

4 Divide the rice among four serving bowls. Cut the chicken fillets into long thick strips, then arrange on top of the rice. Shake the dressing well and drizzle over the chicken and serve with the chargrilled vegetables.

note: Allow 5 minutes for the chargrill pan to heat evenly to medium heat. Do not cook on a smoking hot grill or the chicken will singe, overcooking the outside.

chicken and vegetable stir-fry

PREP TIME: 20 MINUTES +
 2 HOURS MARINATING
COOKING TIME: 20 MINUTES
SERVES 4

1 tablespoon soy sauce
2 garlic cloves, crushed
1 teaspoon grated fresh ginger
1 1/2 teaspoons sesame oil
600 g (1 lb 5 oz) chicken thigh fillets, cut in half lengthways, then across the grain into 6 pieces
2 tablespoons peanut oil
1 onion, cut into 16 wedges
150 g (5 1/2 oz) snowpeas (mangetout), cut in half on the diagonal
250 g (9 oz) bok choy (pak choi)
115 g (4 oz) baby corn, sliced in half on the diagonal
4 tablespoons chopped fresh coriander (cilantro)
2 spring onions (scallions), thinly sliced on the diagonal

Stir-fry sauce

3 tablespoons oyster sauce
3 tablespoons chicken stock
2 teaspoons soy sauce
1 teaspoon cornflour (cornstarch)

NUTRITION PER SERVE: Fat 15 g; Carbohydrate 15 g; Protein 29 g; Dietary Fibre 4.5 g; Cholesterol 66 mg; 1135 kJ (270 Cal)

1 Mix together the soy sauce, garlic, ginger and 1/2 teaspoon sesame oil in a non-metallic bowl. Add the chicken and stir to coat well. Cover and marinate in the fridge for 2 hours.

2 In a separate bowl, mix all the stir-fry sauce ingredients together until the cornflour is incorporated.

3 Heat a wok over high heat and add 1 tablespoon peanut oil and the remaining sesame oil. When hot, add the chicken in batches and stir-fry until just cooked through. Add a little more oil if required. Remove from the wok.

4 Heat the remaining peanut oil in the wok. Add the onion, stir-fry for 2–3 minutes, then add the snowpeas, bok choy and baby corn and stir-fry for 3 minutes. Add the stir-fry sauce and the chicken with any juices. Stir well and cook for about 3 minutes, or until the sauce has thickened to lightly coat the chicken and vegetables. Remove from the heat, and stir in the coriander and spring onion. Season and serve with rice.

stir-fried chicken with chilli caramel sauce

PREP TIME: 10 MINUTES +
 4 HOURS MARINATING
COOKING TIME: 20 MINUTES
SERVES 4

1/2 teaspoon five-spice powder
2 tablespoons grated fresh ginger
2 tablespoons soy sauce
60 ml (1/4 cup) Chinese rice wine or dry sherry
4 garlic cloves, crushed
800 g (1 lb 12 oz) chicken thigh fillets, cubed
4 tablespoons soft brown sugar
3 tablespoons rice vinegar
2 tablespoons sweet chilli sauce
2 tablespoons fish sauce
3 tablespoons chicken stock
3 tablespoons peanut oil
1 small red chilli, seeded and finely chopped
3 tablespoons coriander (cilantro), finely chopped
4 spring onions (scallions), thinly sliced on the diagonal, to garnish

NUTRITION PER SERVE: Fat 27.5 g; Carbohydrate 16 g; Protein 39.5 g; Dietary Fibre 2 g; Cholesterol 174.5 mg; 2010 kJ (480 Cal)

1 Put the five-spice, ginger, soy sauce, wine and half the garlic in a glass or ceramic bowl, add 1 teaspoon salt and 1/2 teaspoon ground black pepper, then stir together. Add the chicken, stir to coat, then cover and marinate in the refrigerator for at least 4 hours. Glass and ceramic are ideal for marinating because metal reacts with acids and plastic absorbs strong flavours.

2 In a small bowl or jug, combine the brown sugar, rice vinegar, sweet chilli sauce, fish sauce and chicken stock.

3 Heat the wok and add 2 tablespoons oil. When the oil starts to smoke, add the chicken in batches and stir-fry for about 3–4 minutes, until golden brown. Remove each batch and keep warm while you cook the rest.

4 Reduce the heat slightly and heat the remaining oil in the wok. Add the chilli and remaining garlic, and cook for 30 seconds. Pour in the sauce mixture and allow it to bubble until reduced, syrupy and caramelised. This will take about 3–5 minutes. When the sauce is thoroughly reduced and caramelised, return the chicken to the wok, without any of the accumulated juices, and cook for 1 minute to coat the chicken in the sauce and heat through. Stir in the coriander. Garnish with the spring onion before serving.

chicken cacciatora

PREP TIME: 20 MINUTES +
10 MINUTES STANDING
COOKING TIME: 1 HOUR 15 MINUTES
SERVES 4

1 kg (2 lb 4 oz) ripe tomatoes, preferably vine-ripened, or 2 x 400 g (14 oz) tins chopped tomatoes
1.5 kg (3 lb 5 oz) chicken, cut into 8 pieces
2 tablespoons olive oil
2 onions, sliced
2 garlic cloves, finely chopped
2 tablespoons tomato paste (purée)
1 teaspoon sugar
1 1/2 tablespoons finely chopped rosemary
2 bay leaves
185 ml (3/4 cup) dry white wine
125 ml (1/2 cup) chicken stock
1 tablespoon lemon juice
80 g (1/2 cup) kalamata olives (optional)

NUTRITION PER SERVE: Fat 35 g; Carbohydrate 14.5 g; Protein 42 g; Dietary Fibre 4 g; Cholesterol 187.5 mg; 2340 kJ (570 Cal)

1 If you are using fresh tomatoes, peel and seed them and cut into smallish dice.

2 Cut any excess skin and fat from the chicken pieces, and season them well with salt and black pepper. Heat the oil in a heavy-based frying pan over medium–high heat and cook the chicken pieces a few at a time until golden brown. Remove from the pan.

3 Add the onion to the pan and cook over low heat until wilted and just starting to caramelize (this will take about 10 minutes). Don't let it brown too much. Add the tomato, garlic, tomato paste, sugar, herbs, wine and stock. Bring to the boil, then reduce the heat and simmer, uncovered, for 15 minutes, or until reduced by half.

4 Add the chicken pieces to the sauce and season well with salt and pepper. Add the lemon juice, then cover and cook over very low heat for 30 minutes. Add the olives, then remove from the heat and leave, covered, for 10 minutes. Serve with noodles.

creamy chicken with tarragon and mustard

PREP TIME: 25 MINUTES + OVERNIGHT MARINATING
COOKING TIME: 1 HOUR 40 MINUTES
SERVES 4

1.5 kg (3 lb 5 oz) chicken, cut into 8 pieces
2 1/2 tablespoons wholegrain mustard
1 teaspoon chopped tarragon, plus extra to garnish
2 tablespoons butter
2 teaspoons olive oil
85 g (3 oz) streaky bacon or mild pancetta, finely chopped
3 French shallots, finely chopped (see Note)
2 garlic cloves, finely chopped
1 tablespoon plain (all-purpose) flour
185 ml (3/4 cup) dry white wine
315 ml (1 1/4 cups) chicken stock
125 ml (1/2 cup) cream

NUTRITION PER SERVE: Fat 52 g; Carbohydrate 4.5 g; Protein 42 g; Dietary Fibre 1 g; Cholesterol 254 mg; 2835 kJ (675 Cal)

1 Put the chicken pieces in a glass or ceramic dish. Mix 1 1/2 tablespoons mustard with the chopped tarragon and rub the mixture all over the chicken pieces. Cover and refrigerate overnight.

2 Preheat the oven to 180°C (350°F/Gas 4). Melt the butter and oil in a frying pan over medium–high heat and brown the chicken joints in two batches until the skin is golden. Transfer to a lidded ovenproof casserole dish.

3 Add the bacon, shallots and garlic to the pan and cook until the bacon just starts to brown. Stir in the flour and cook for 1 minute. Add the wine, stock and remaining mustard and cook for about 5 minutes, until the sauce is smooth. Pour over the chicken, then cover and bake for 1 hour 10 minutes.

4 Remove the chicken from the pan. Stir the cream into the sauce, then reduce the sauce over high heat until it reaches a coating consistency.

5 Add the chicken to the sauce and stir until well coated. Serve on a platter with the sauce poured over the chicken. Garnish with the extra tarragon. Serve with mashed potato and green vegetables or salad.

note: French shallots are also known as eschallots. They are a close relative of the onion, but with a milder, delicate flavour. They grow in clusters and are joined with a common root end. French shallots have a copper-coloured skin and elongated bulb.

coq au vin

PREP TIME: 20 MINUTES +
   OVERNIGHT MARINATING
COOKING TIME: 1 HOUR 10 MINUTES
SERVES 4

1.5 kg (3 lb 5 oz) chicken, cut into 8 pieces
500 ml (2 cups) good-quality red wine
bouquet garni (including thyme, bay leaf
   and parsley)
1 tablespoon olive oil
125 g (4½ oz) speck, skin discarded,
   cut into strips
1 onion, chopped
2 garlic cloves, crushed
1 tablespoon brandy
1 tablespoon plain (all-purpose) flour
1 tablespoon tomato paste (purée)
500 ml (2 cups) chicken stock
12 baby onions, peeled
3 tablespoons unsalted butter, chilled
12 button mushrooms
chopped parsley, to serve

NUTRITION PER SERVE: Fat 44 g; Carbohydrate 10 g; Protein 43.5 g; Dietary Fibre 3 g; Cholesterol 226 mg; 2935 kJ (700 Cal)

1 Place the chicken pieces in a glass or ceramic dish and add the red wine and bouquet garni. Cover and marinate in the refrigerator overnight.

2 In a heavy, cast-iron pan, heat the oil over medium–high heat and add the speck. Cook until it renders some of its fat and is golden brown. Drain on paper towels, leaving the fat in the pan.

3 Pat the chicken dry and retain the marinade and bouquet garni. Fry the chicken pieces three or four at a time until they start to change colour. Remove from the pan. Add the onion and cook for 1 minute. Add the garlic and brandy and cook until all the liquid has evaporated. Stir in the flour and the tomato paste. Deglaze the pan with the reserved marinade and bouquet garni and reduce the liquid by half. Return the chicken to the pan, then add enough stock to cover the chicken pieces. Bring to the boil, then reduce the heat and simmer, covered, for 30 minutes.

4 While the chicken is cooking, bring a saucepan of salted water to the boil and blanch the baby onions for 8 minutes. Drain. Melt 20 g (½ oz) of butter in a saucepan, add the button mushrooms and cook for 4 minutes, then remove from the pan.

5 When the chicken has been cooking for 30 minutes, add the mushrooms and baby onions to the pan and cook for another 10 minutes.

6 Using a slotted spoon, transfer the chicken and vegetables to a platter. Remove the bouquet garni. Return the pan to the heat and boil vigorously to reduce by almost half. Then cut the remaining butter into small cubes and whisk it one piece at a time into the sauce until the sauce is rich and glossy. Strain the sauce over the chicken and garnish with the parsley.

chicken tagine

PREP TIME: 20 MINUTES
COOKING TIME: 1 HOUR 15 MINUTES
SERVES 4

1 teaspoon cumin seeds
1 teaspoon coriander seeds
1 teaspoon ground ginger
1 teaspoon ground turmeric
1 teaspoon ground cinnamon
pinch of saffron threads
1/2 teaspoon chilli flakes
1 kg (2 lb 4 oz) chicken thigh fillets, cut into halves
2 tablespoons olive oil
2 onions, chopped
4 garlic cloves, crushed
500 ml (2 cups) chicken stock
2 large tomatoes, peeled, seeded and roughly chopped
80 g (1/4 cup) fresh dates, pitted and quartered
85 g (1/3 cup) dried apricots (if big, cut in half)
80 g (1/2 cup) blanched almonds, toasted
chopped coriander (cilantro), to garnish

NUTRITION PER SERVE: Fat 30.5 g; Carbohydrate 22 g; Protein 60.5 g; Dietary Fibre 7.5 g; Cholesterol 173 mg; 2515 kJ (600 Cal)

1 Heat a large frying pan over low heat and add the cumin and coriander seeds, ginger, turmeric, cinnamon, saffron and chilli flakes. Shake the pan over the heat for 1–2 minutes, or until the spices are aromatic, then transfer to a mortar and pestle or spice grinder, and grind to a fine powder.

2 Remove all the fat and sinew from the chicken. Sprinkle with the dry spice mixture, retaining any that is left. Heat the oil in the frying pan over medium heat and cook the chicken pieces in batches on both sides until lightly golden. Drain well on paper towels.

3 In the same pan, cook the onion over medium heat for 5 minutes, or until golden. Add the garlic, stock, tomato and remaining spice mixture. Add the chicken, bring to the boil, then cover, reduce the heat and simmer for 25 minutes. Add the dates and apricots and cook for 25 minutes, or until the mixture thickens slightly. Season, then stir in the nuts. Garnish with coriander, and serve with steamed couscous. Traditionally served with harissa on the side.

indian butter chicken

PREP TIME: 20 MINUTES
COOKING TIME: 1 HOUR
SERVES 4

2 tablespoons tandoori spice blend
100 g (3 1/2 oz) butter
1 tablespoon canola oil
800 g (1 lb 12 oz) chicken thigh fillets, trimmed of all fat and sinew, cut into chunks
1 onion, finely diced
2 large garlic cloves, crushed
1 teaspoon ground cumin
1 teaspoon paprika
1 1/2 teaspoons garam masala
2 tablespoons tomato paste (purée)
250 ml (1 cup) chicken stock
250 ml (1 cup) thick (double/heavy) cream
1 teaspoon sugar
1 tablespoon ground almonds
80 g (1/3 cup) plain yoghurt
3 tablespoons finely chopped coriander (cilantro)

NUTRITION PER SERVE: Fat 56.5 g; Carbohydrate 8.5 g; Protein 46.5 g; Dietary Fibre 3 g; Cholesterol 269.5 mg; 3035 kJ (725 Cal)

1 Heat a large, heavy-based saucepan over low heat, add the tandoori spice blend and dry-fry, shaking the pan occasionally, for 1–2 minutes, or until fragrant. Be careful the spices don't burn. Transfer to a small bowl.

2 Melt 1 tablespoon of the butter with the canola oil in the saucepan over medium heat. Add the chicken in batches and cook until golden. Remove from the pan.

3 Melt the remaining butter in the same pan. Add the onion, garlic, cumin, paprika and garam masala and cook for 2 minutes, or until fragrant. Add the tandoori spice blend and the tomato paste and cook for another 2 minutes. Add the chicken stock, cream and sugar, then reduce the heat and simmer for 15 minutes, or until the sauce has thickened slightly.

4 Stir in the ground almonds and the chicken, along with any juices, and cook for 15 minutes, or until the chicken is cooked through and tender. Remove from the heat, stir in the yoghurt and coriander and season well. Serve with steamed basmati rice.

steamed chicken breast with asian greens and soy mushroom sauce

PREP TIME: 10 MINUTES + 20 MINUTES SOAKING + 1 HOUR MARINATING
COOKING TIME: 20 MINUTES
SERVES 4

8–10 g (1/4 oz) dried Chinese mushrooms
2 tablespoons light soy sauce
2 tablespoons rice wine
1/2 teaspoon sesame oil
1 tablespoon finely sliced fresh ginger
4 chicken breast fillets (about 200 g/7 oz each), trimmed
450 g (1 lb) bok choy (pak choi), ends removed and cut lengthways into quarters (see Note)
125 ml (1/2 cup) chicken stock
1 tablespoon cornflour (cornstarch)

NUTRITION PER SERVE: Fat 5.5 g; Carbohydrate 4.5 g; Protein 45.5 g; Dietary Fibre 2 g; Cholesterol 95 mg; 1085 kJ (260 Cal)

1 Soak the mushrooms in 60 ml (1/4 cup) boiling water for 20 minutes. Drain and reserve the liquid. Discard the stalks and slice the caps thinly.

2 Combine the soy sauce, rice wine, sesame oil and ginger in a non-metallic dish. Add the chicken to the marinade and turn to coat. Cover and marinate for 1 hour.

3 Line a bamboo steamer with baking paper. Place the chicken on top, reserving the marinade. Bring water to the boil in a wok, then place the steamer in the wok. Cover and steam for 6 minutes, then turn the chicken over and steam for a further 6 minutes. Place the bok choy on top of the chicken and steam for 2–3 minutes.

4 Meanwhile, place the marinade, mushrooms and their soaking liquid in a small saucepan and bring to the boil. Put the cornflour in a small bowl and add enough stock to make a smooth paste. Add the paste and remaining stock to the mushroom mixture and stir over medium heat for 2 minutes, or until the sauce thickens.

5 Place some bok choy and a chicken fillet on each serving plate, then pour on a little sauce. Serve with rice.

note: Bok choy is a member of the cabbage family with a slightly mustardy taste. It has fleshy white stems and dark green leaves.

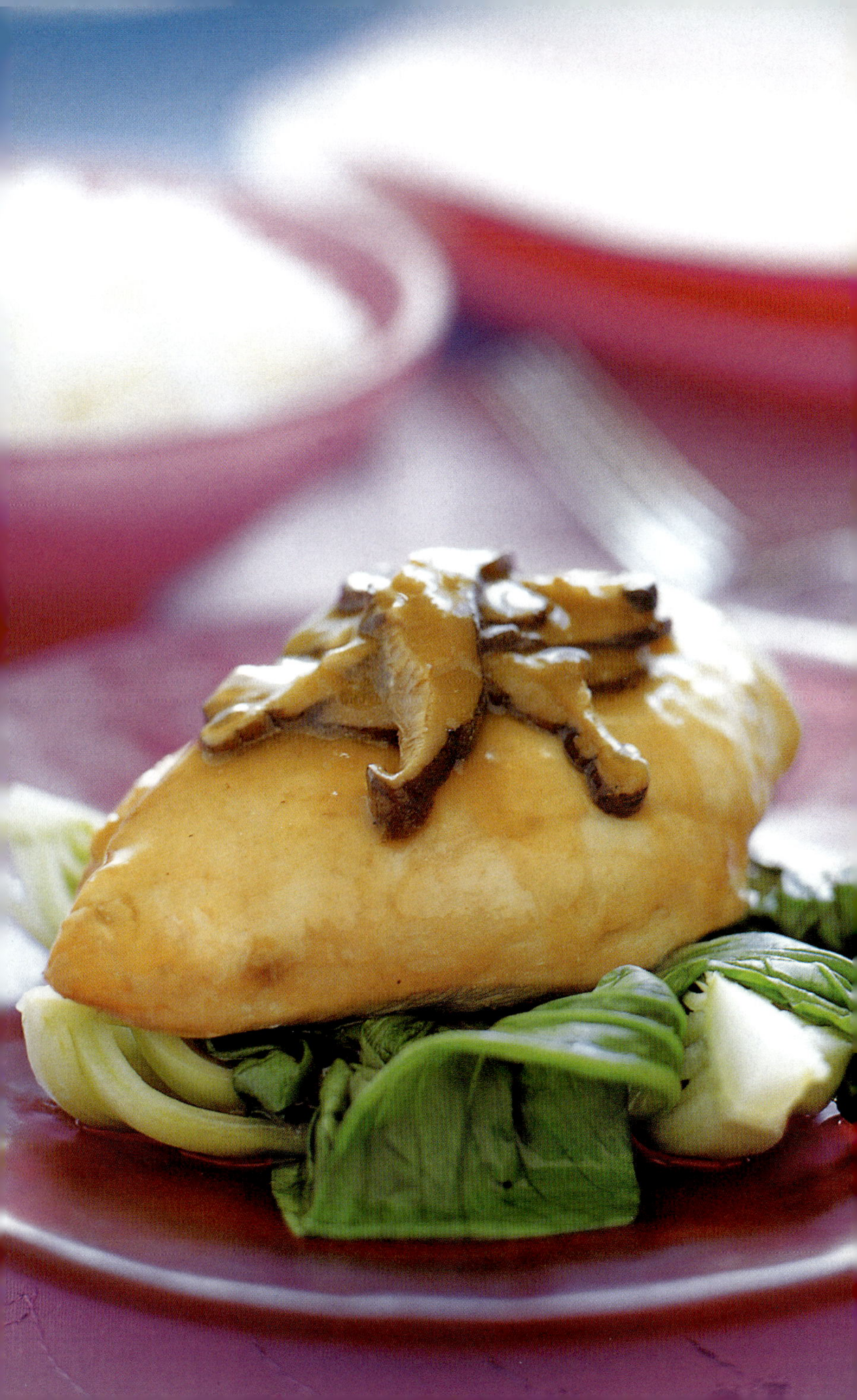

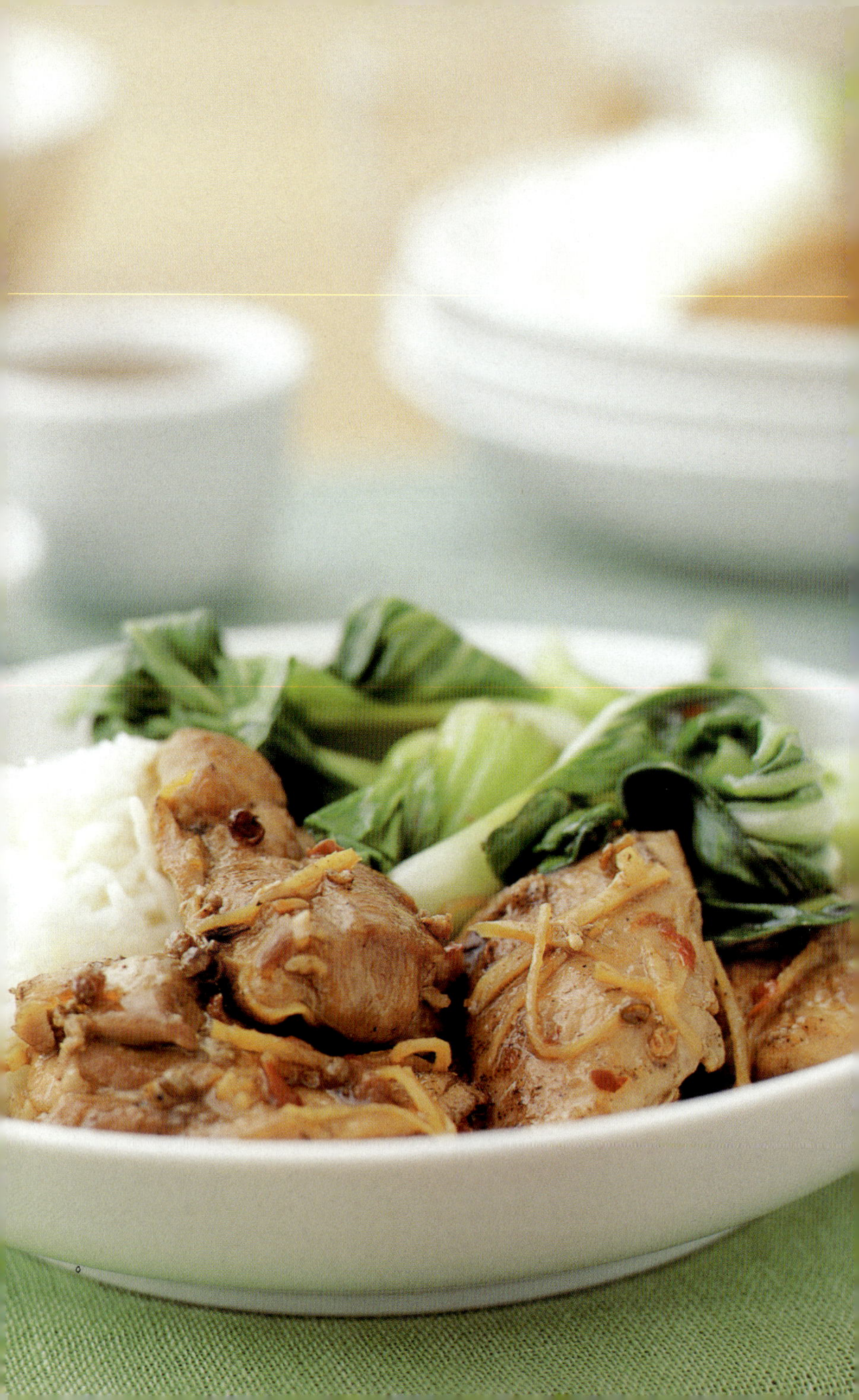

sichuan chicken

PREP TIME: 10 MINUTES
COOKING TIME: 25 MINUTES
SERVES 4

1/4 teaspoon five-spice powder
750 g (1 lb 10 oz) chicken thigh fillets, halved
2 tablespoons peanut oil
1 tablespoon julienned fresh ginger
1 teaspoon Sichuan peppercorns, crushed
1 teaspoon chilli bean paste (see Note)
2 tablespoons light soy sauce
1 tablespoon Chinese rice wine or dry sherry
250 g (1 1/4 cups) jasmine rice
600 g (1 lb 5 oz) baby bok choy (pak choi), leaves separated

NUTRITION PER SERVE: Fat 23.5 g; Carbohydrate 52 g; Protein 42 g; Dietary Fibre 2.5 g; Cholesterol 163 mg; 2465 kJ (590 Cal)

1 Sprinkle the five-spice powder over the chicken. Heat a wok until very hot, add half the oil and swirl to coat. Add the chicken and cook for 2 minutes each side, or until browned. Remove from the wok.

2 Reduce the heat to medium and cook the ginger for 30 seconds. Add the peppercorns and chilli bean paste. Return the chicken to the wok, add the soy sauce, wine and 125 ml (1/2 cup) water, then simmer for 15–20 minutes, or until cooked.

3 Meanwhile, bring a saucepan of water to the boil. Add the rice and cook for 12 minutes, stirring occasionally. Drain well.

4 Heat the remaining oil in a saucepan. Add the bok choy and toss gently for 1 minute, or until the leaves wilt and the stems are tender. Serve with the chicken and rice.

note: Chilli bean paste (also known as toban djan) is sometimes called red bean chilli paste, hot bean paste or chilli bean sauce. It is a paste made from fermented and salted soy beans, then augmented with chillies. Available in Asian grocers and large supermarkets.

honey chicken

PREP TIME: 10 MINUTES +
10 MINUTES STANDING
COOKING TIME: 20 MINUTES
SERVES 4

1 kg (2 lb 4 oz) boned chicken breasts, skin on
2 1/2 tablespoons cornflour (cornstarch)
125 g (1 cup) self-raising flour
1 egg, lightly beaten
peanut oil, for deep-frying, plus 1 tablespoon for stir-frying
1 tablespoon soy sauce
3 x 2 cm (1 1/4 x 3/4 inch) piece fresh ginger, finely chopped
4 tablespoons honey
2 spring onions (scallions), thinly sliced on the diagonal, to garnish

NUTRITION PER SERVE: Fat 33.5 g; Carbohydrate 52 g; Protein 45 g; Dietary Fibre 1.5 g; Cholesterol 193 mg; 2860 kJ (685 Cal)

1 Cut the chicken into small bite-sized pieces and put them in a bowl with 1 1/2 tablespoons of the cornflour. Shake to coat well, then leave for 10 minutes.

2 In a separate bowl, mix the flour and egg with 310 ml (1 1/4 cups) cold water until you have a loose batter.

3 Fill a wok with enough oil to deep-fry the chicken pieces, then heat to 190°C (375°F/Gas 5), or until a cube of bread dropped into the oil browns in 10 seconds. Dip the chicken in the batter, allowing the excess to drip off. Fry the chicken in batches until crisp and golden. Drain on paper towels.

4 Mix the soy sauce and remaining cornflour in a small bowl.

5 Drain the oil from the wok and wipe the wok clean. Heat the remaining oil, add the ginger and stir-fry for 1 minute. Add the honey and, when it is heated through, add the chicken pieces and coat well. Stir in the soy and cornflour mixture and cook for 1 more minute. Pile into a bowl and garnish with the spring onion.

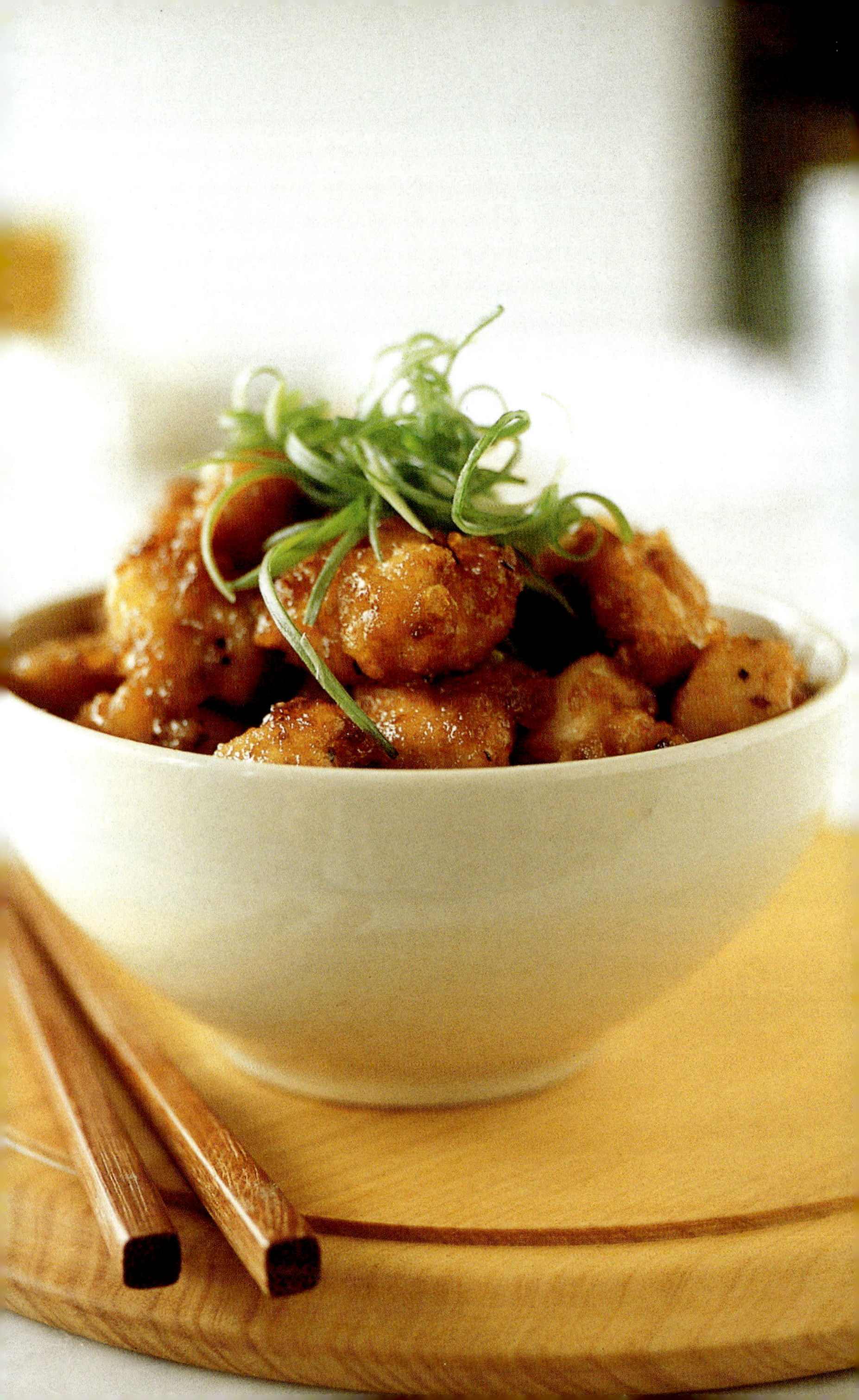

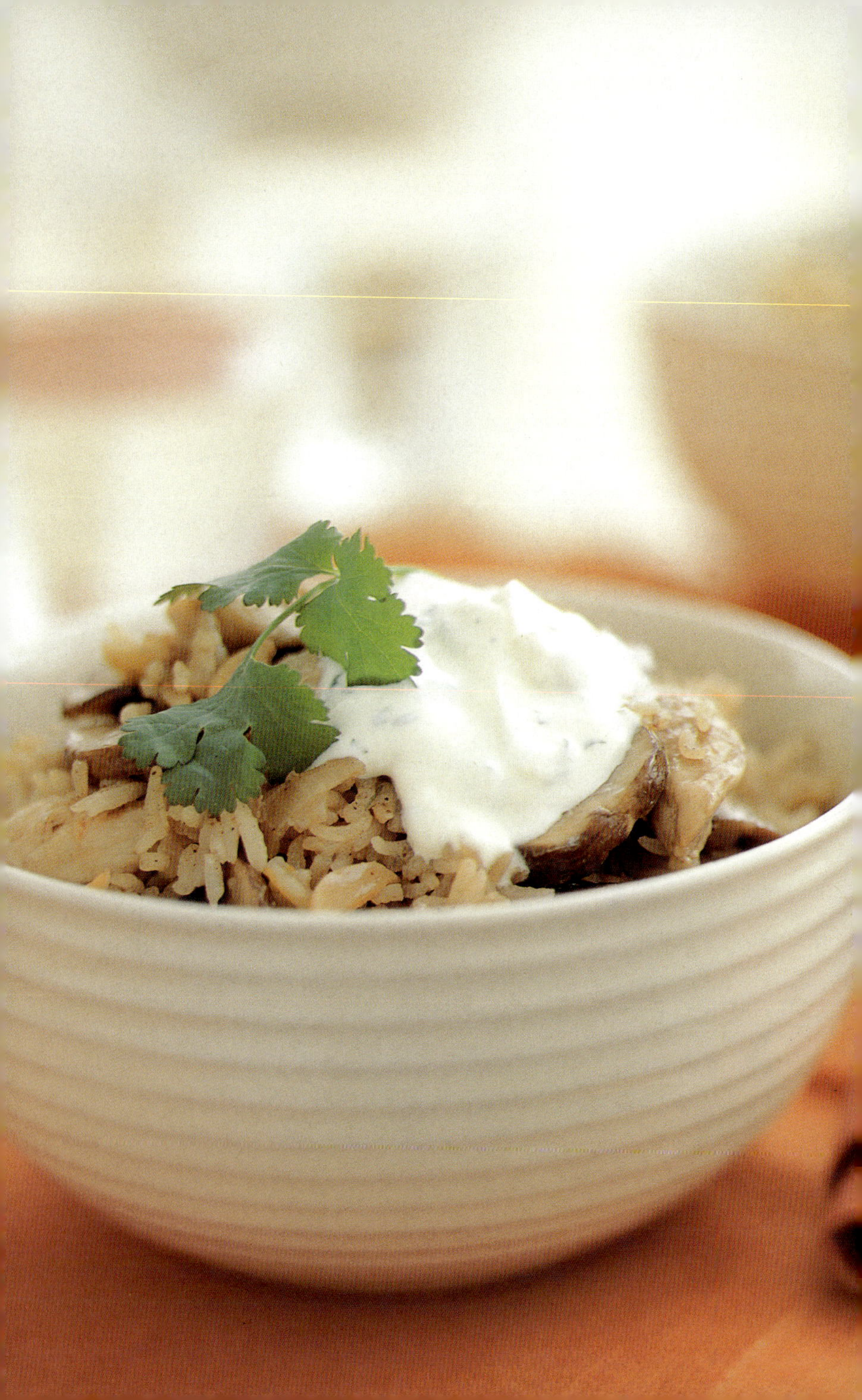

chicken and mushroom pilau

PREP TIME: 15 MINUTES +
  30 MINUTES STANDING
COOKING TIME: 35 MINUTES
SERVES 4

300 g (1 1/2 cups) basmati rice
2 tablespoons oil
1 large onion, chopped
3–4 garlic cloves, crushed
1 tablespoon finely chopped fresh ginger
500 g (1 lb 2 oz) chicken tenderloin fillets, trimmed and cut into small pieces
300 g (10 1/2 oz) Swiss brown mushrooms, sliced
90 g (3/4 cup) slivered almonds, toasted
1 1/2–2 teaspoons garam masala, dry roasted (see Note)
125 g (1/2 cup) plain yoghurt
1 tablespoon finely chopped coriander (cilantro) leaves, plus extra, to garnish

NUTRITION PER SERVE: Fat 31.5 g; Carbohydrate 67 g; Protein 38 g; Dietary Fibre 6 g; Cholesterol 112.5 mg; 2933 kJ (698 Cal)

1 Rinse the rice under cold water until the water runs clear. Drain and leave for 30 minutes. Heat the oil in a large saucepan over medium heat and stir in the onion, garlic and ginger. Cook, covered, for 5 minutes, or until the onion is browned. Increase the heat to high, add the chicken and cook, stirring, for 3–4 minutes, or until the chicken is lightly browned.

2 Stir in the mushrooms, almonds and garam masala. Cook, covered, for 3 minutes, or until the mushrooms are soft. Remove the lid and cook, stirring, for 2 minutes, or until the liquid evaporates. Remove the chicken pieces from the pan.

3 Add the rice to the pan and stir for 30 seconds, or until well coated in the mushroom and onion mixture. Pour in 375 ml (1 1/2 cups) water and bring to the boil, stirring frequently to prevent the ingredients catching on the bottom of the pan. Cook for 2 minutes, or until most of the water has evaporated. Return the chicken to the pan, reduce the heat to low and steam, covered, for 15 minutes, or until the rice is cooked.

4 Meanwhile, combine the yoghurt and chopped coriander in a small bowl. Fluff the rice with a fork, then divide among serving bowls. Top with a dollop of the yoghurt mixture and garnish with coriander leaves.

note: Garam masala is a mixture of ground spices that usually includes cinnamon, black pepper, coriander, cumin, cardamom, cloves and mace. Available in the spice aisle of the supermarket.

chicken breast stuffed with tomato, goat's cheese and asparagus

PREP TIME: 15 MINUTES
COOKING TIME: 20 MINUTES
SERVES 4

200 g (7 oz) asparagus spears, trimmed and halved
4 large chicken breast fillets
100 g (3½ oz) semi-dried (sun-blushed) tomatoes
100 g (3½ oz) mild goat's cheese, sliced
50 g (1¾ oz) butter
375 ml (1½ cups) chicken stock
2 zucchini (courgettes), cut into 5 cm (2 inch) batons
250 ml (1 cup) cream
8 spring onions (scallions), thinly sliced

NUTRITION PER SERVE: Fat 63.5 g; Carbohydrate 10 g; Protein 90 g; Dietary Fibre 4 g; Cholesterol 377 mg; 4045 kJ (965 Cal)

1 Cook asparagus in a saucepan of boiling water for 1–2 minutes until tender, then drain.

2 Pound each chicken breast between two sheets of plastic wrap with a mallet or rolling pin until 1 cm (½ inch) thick. Divide the tomato, goat's cheese and most of the asparagus pieces among the breasts. Roll up tightly lengthways, securing with toothpicks.

3 Heat the butter in a large frying pan over medium heat. Add the chicken, and brown on all sides. Pour in the stock, then reduce the heat to low. Cook, covered, for 10 minutes, or until the chicken is cooked through. Remove the chicken and keep warm.

4 Meanwhile, bring a saucepan of lightly salted water to the boil. Add the zucchini and remaining asparagus and cook for 2 minutes, or until just tender. Remove from the pan.

5 Whisk the cream into the stock in the frying pan. Add the spring onion and simmer over medium–low heat for 4 minutes, or until reduced and thickened.

6 To serve, cut each chicken roll in half on the diagonal and place on serving plates. Spoon on the sauce and serve with the greens.

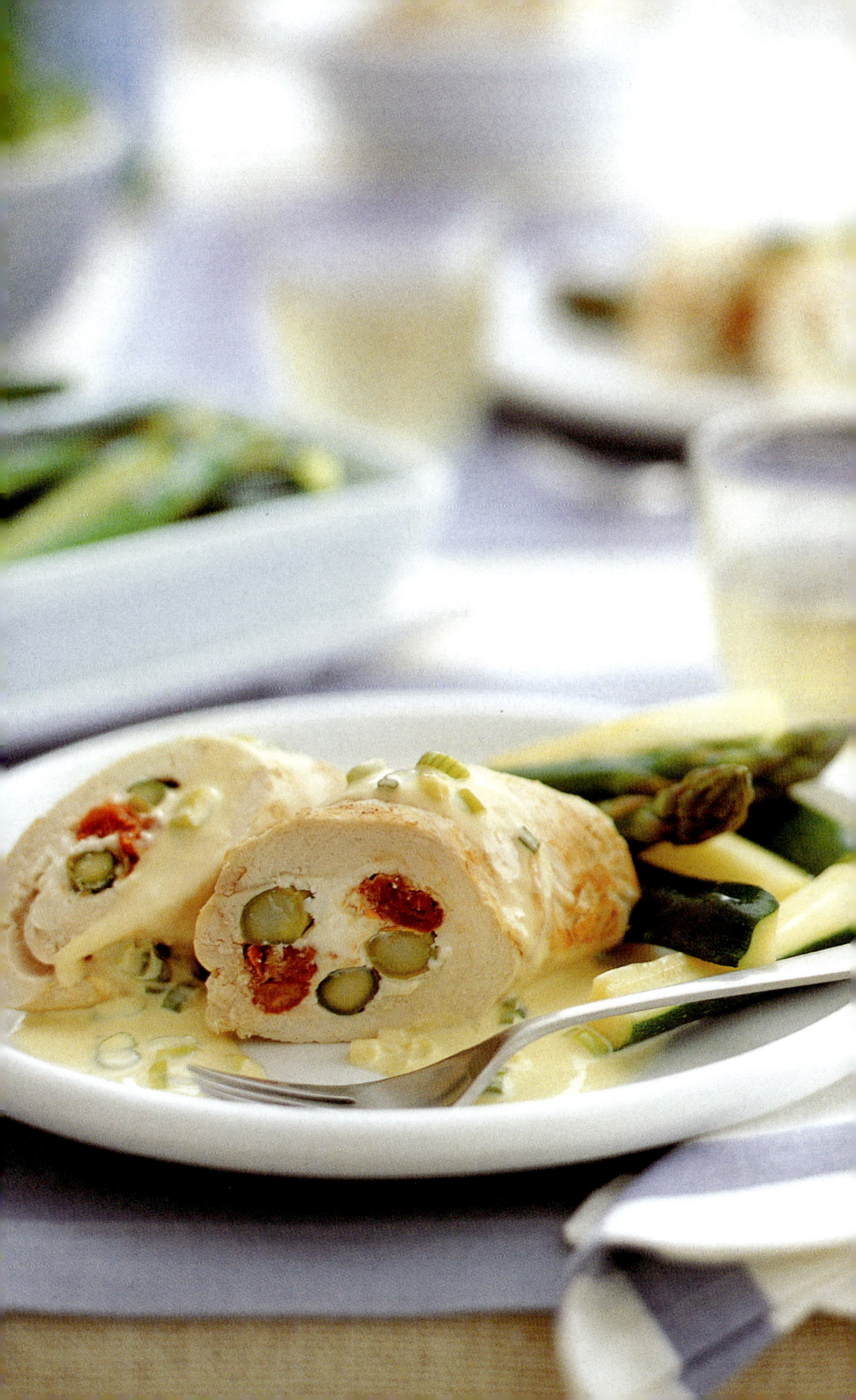

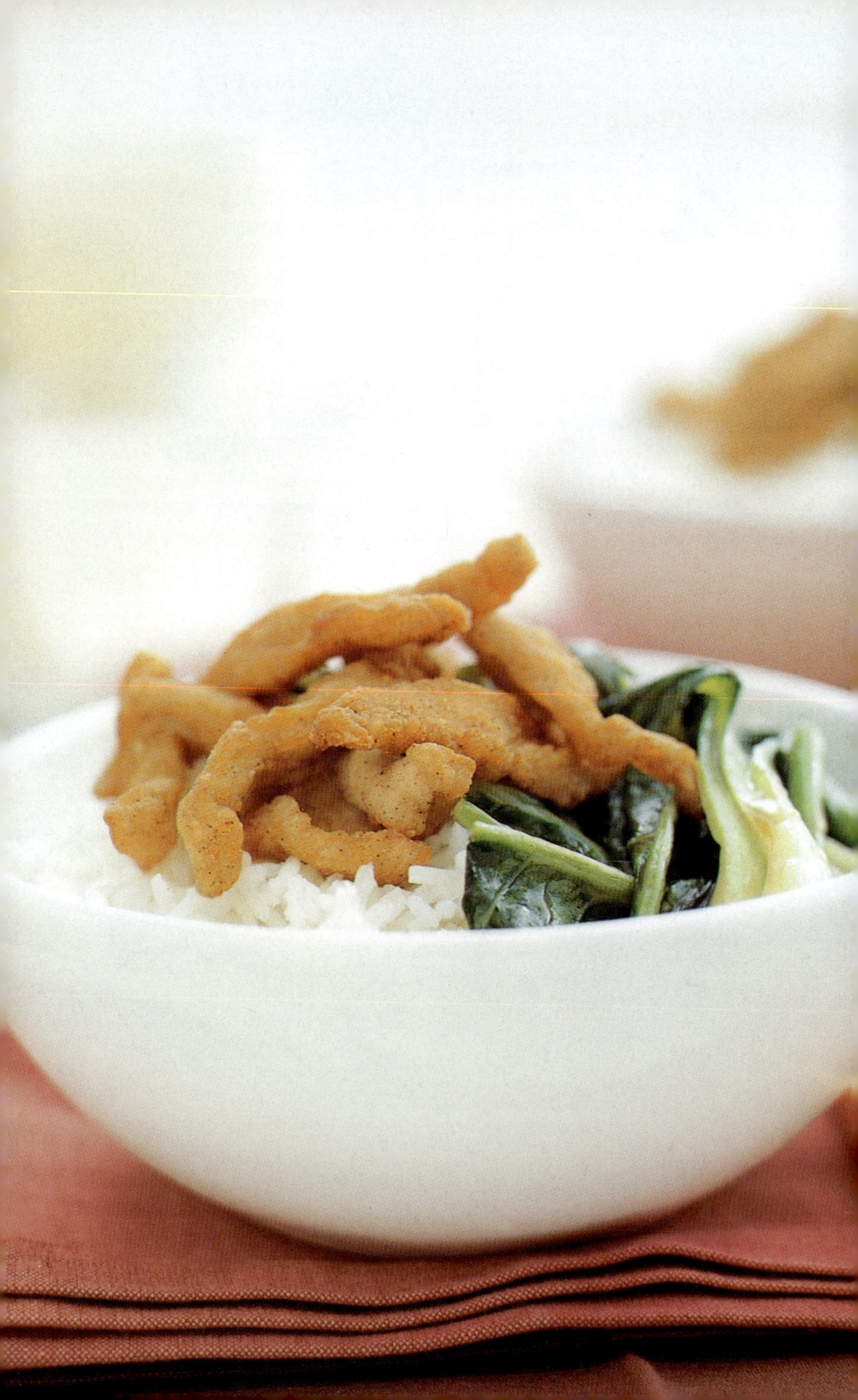

salt and pepper chicken with asian greens and oyster sauce

PREP TIME: 15 MINUTES
COOKING TIME: 20 MINUTES
SERVES 4

3 tablespoons plain (all-purpose) flour
3/4 teaspoon five-spice powder
1 1/2 teaspoons fine sea salt
1 teaspoon ground white pepper
750 g (1 lb 10 oz) chicken breast fillets, cut into thin strips
145 ml (5 fl oz) peanut oil
1.25 kg (2 lb 12 oz) mixed Asian greens
125 ml (1/2 cup) oyster sauce

NUTRITION PER SERVE: Fat 32.5 g; Carbohydrate 68 g; Protein 50 g; Dietary Fibre 5 g; Cholesterol 123.5 mg; 3195 kJ (765 Cal)

1 Combine the flour, five-spice powder, salt and pepper in a bowl. Toss the chicken strips in the flour until well coated. Heat 60 ml (1/4 cup) of the oil in a frying pan over medium–high heat. Add the chicken in three batches and cook, turning, until browned. Drain on crumpled paper towels and keep warm.

2 Heat the remaining oil and cook the mixed Asian greens over medium–high heat for 1–2 minutes. Add the oyster sauce and toss through. Serve the chicken with the greens. Add some steamed jasmine rice if desired.

pictured: salt and pepper chicken with asian greens and oyster sauce

spicy roast chicken

PREP TIME: 20 MINUTES
COOKING TIME: 1 HOUR
SERVES 4–6

1.5 kg (3 lb) chicken
3 teaspoons chopped chillies
3 garlic cloves, peeled
2 teaspoons dried green peppercorns, crushed
2 teaspoons soft brown sugar
2 tablespoons soy sauce
2 teaspoons ground turmeric
1 tablespoon lime juice
30 g (1 oz) butter, chopped

NUTRITION PER SERVE (6): Fat 18.5 g; Carbohydrate 2 g; Protein 22.5 g; Dietary Fibre 1 g; Cholesterol 117.5 mg; 1105 kJ (265 Cal)

1 Preheat the oven to 180°C (350°F/Gas 4). Using a large cleaver, cut the chicken in half by cutting down the backbone and along the breastbone. To prevent the wings burning, tuck them underneath. Place the chicken, skin-side-up, on a rack in a baking dish and bake for 30 minutes.

2 Meanwhile, combine the chillies, garlic, peppercorns and sugar in a small food processor or mortar and pestle and process briefly, or pound, until smooth. Add the soy sauce, turmeric and lime juice, and process in short bursts until combined.

3 Brush the spice mixture all over the chicken, dot with the butter pieces and bake for another 25–30 minutes, or until thoroughly cooked. Serve warm or at room temperature, garnished with lime wedges and fresh herbs.

parmesan chicken with quick salsa verde

PREP TIME: 15 MINUTES +
  10 MINUTES REFRIGERATION
COOKING TIME: 15 MINUTES
SERVES 4

3 eggs
30 g (1 cup) loosely packed basil
2 tablespoons capers, rinsed and dried
1 tablespoon Dijon mustard
2 tablespoons freshly grated Parmesan cheese
285 ml (3/4 cup) olive oil
100 g (1 cup) dry breadcrumbs
4 chicken breast fillets
150 g (5 1/2 oz) rocket (arugula) leaves
lemon wedges, to serve

NUTRITION PER SERVE: Fat 47 g; Carbohydrate 18.5 g; Protein 37 g; Dietary Fibre 2 g; Cholesterol 234.5 mg; 2685 kJ (640 Cal)

1 To make the salsa verde, put 1 egg in a saucepan of cold water, bring to the boil and cook for 1 minute. Remove from the heat and refresh under cold water. Peel, then place in a food processor with the basil, capers, mustard and 1 tablespoon of the Parmesan cheese, and blend until combined. Gradually add 60 ml (1/4 cup) of the olive oil and process until you have a coarse sauce, taking care not to overmix.

2 Beat the remaining eggs together with 1 tablespoon water. Combine the breadcrumbs with the remaining Parmesan on a plate. Pound each chicken breast between two sheets of plastic wrap with a mallet or rolling pin until 5 mm (1/4 inch) thick. Dip the chicken in the egg mixture, then coat in the breadcrumb mixture. Place on a paper-lined baking tray and refrigerate for 10 minutes, or until needed.

3 Heat the remaining oil in a frying pan over high heat. Cook the chicken breasts in batches for 2–3 minutes each batch, or until golden on both sides and cooked through—keep warm between batches. Serve with the salsa verde, rocket leaves and lemon wedges.

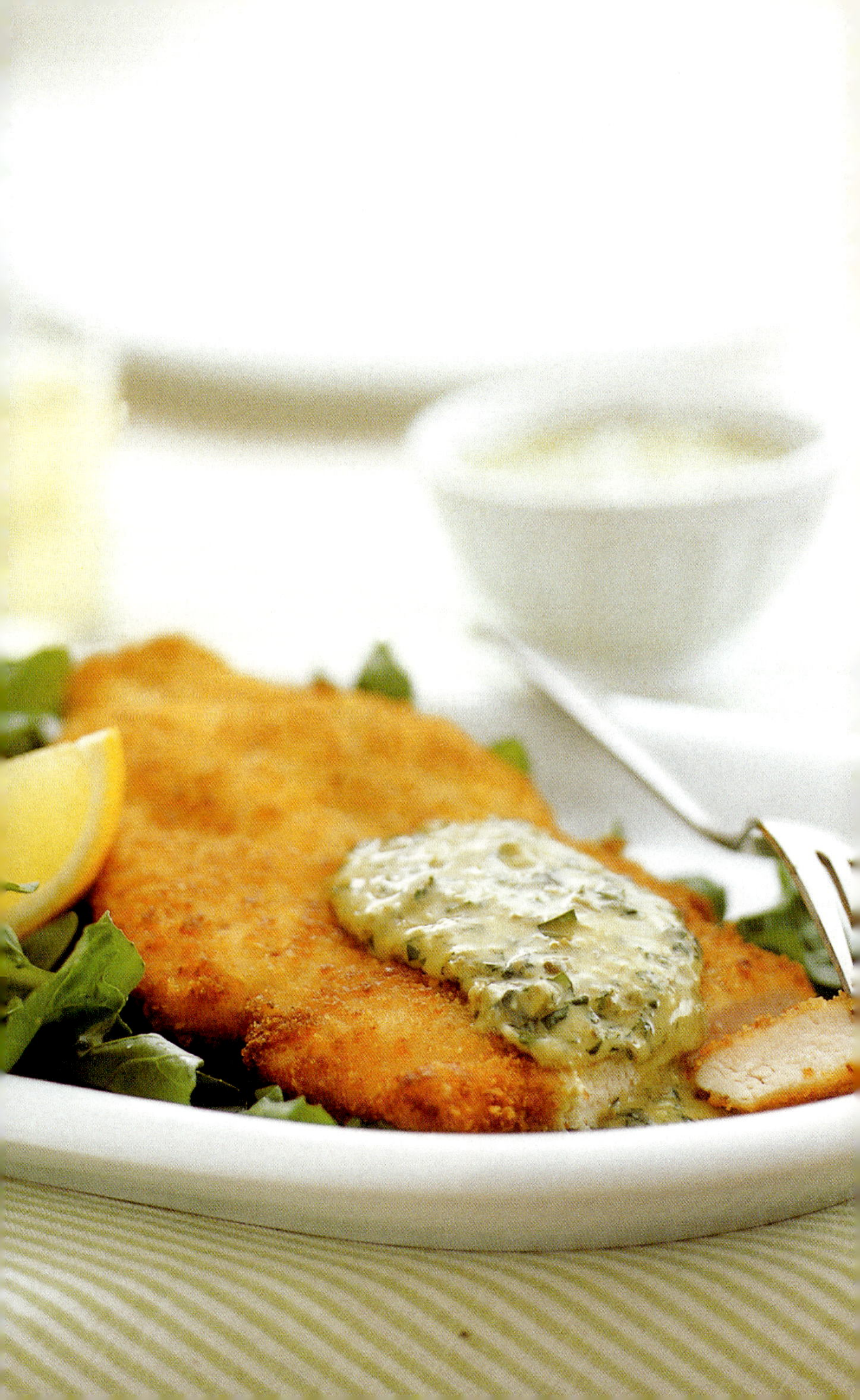

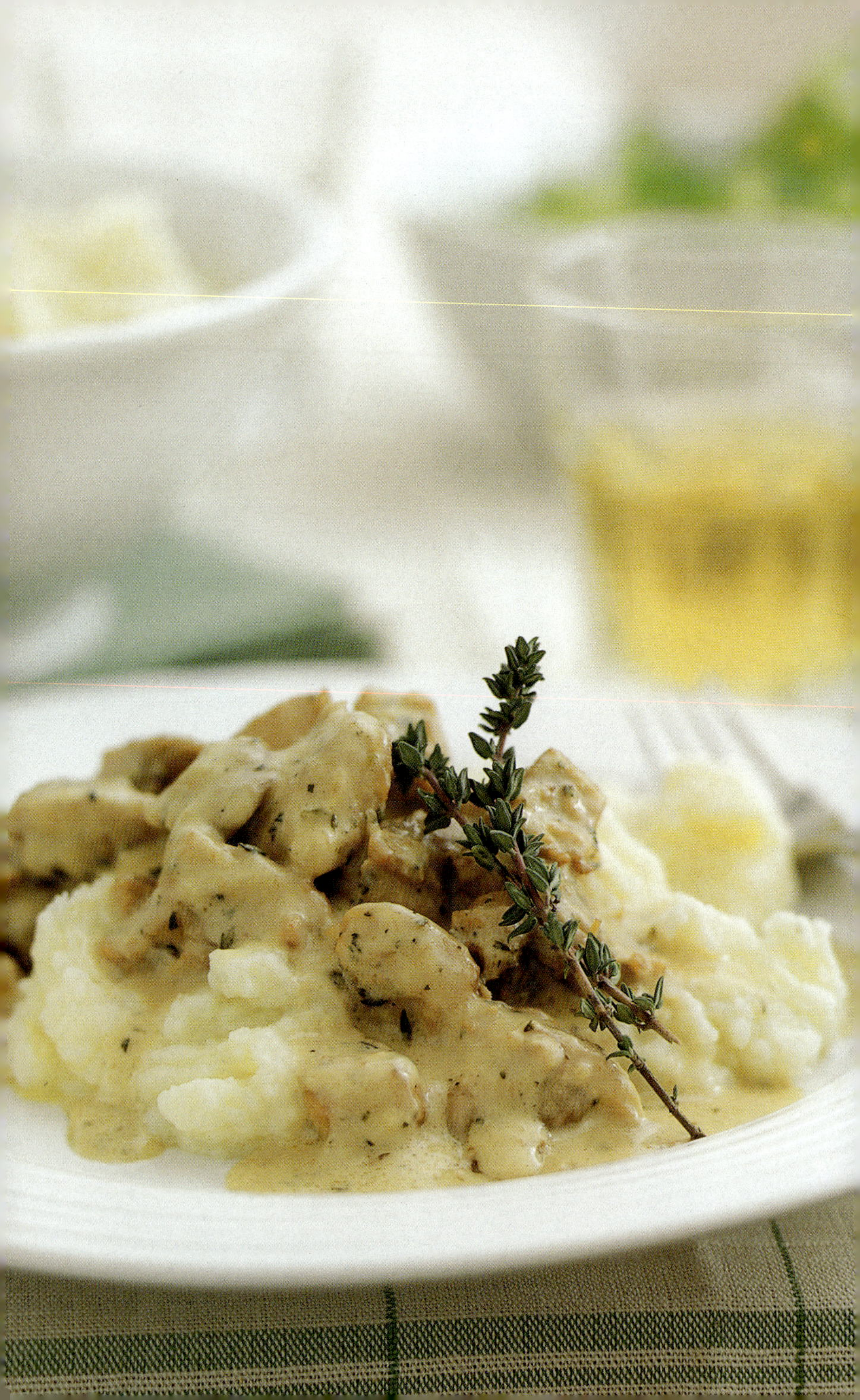

chicken and cider stew with apple and potato mash

PREP TIME: 15 MINUTES
COOKING TIME: 55 MINUTES
SERVES 4

1 kg (2 lb 4 oz) chicken thigh fillets, trimmed and cut into 2 cm (3/4 inch) cubes
1 1/2 tablespoons finely chopped thyme
1 tablespoon oil
90 g (3 1/4 oz) butter
3 French shallots, thinly sliced
375 ml (1 1/2 cups) apple cider
1 kg (2 lb 4 oz) potatoes, peeled and cubed
2 large green apples, peeled, cored and sliced into eighths
170 ml (2/3 cup) cream

NUTRITION PER SERVE: Fat 59.5 g; Carbohydrate 56 g; Protein 54 g; Dietary Fibre 6 g; Cholesterol 333 mg; 4055 kJ (970 Cal)

1 Season the chicken thighs with 2 teaspoons of the thyme and salt and black pepper. Heat the oil and 1 tablespoon of the butter in a large saucepan over medium–high heat. Cook the chicken in two batches for 2–3 minutes, or until evenly browned. Remove from the pan.

2 Add the French shallots and the remaining thyme to the pan and sauté for 2 minutes. Pour in the cider, then bring to the boil, scraping off any sediment that has stuck to the bottom of the pan. Return the chicken to the pan and cover. Reduce the heat to medium–low and cook for 35 minutes, or until the chicken is tender and the sauce has reduced (check occasionally to see if any water needs to be added).

3 Meanwhile, cook the potato and apple in a saucepan of boiling water for 15–20 minutes, or until tender. Drain and return to the pan over low heat for a minute to allow any water to evaporate. Remove from the heat, and mash with a potato masher. Stir in 2 tablespoons of the cream and the remaining butter with a wooden spoon, then season well with salt and pepper.

4 Gently stir the remaining cream into the chicken stew and cook for a further 2–4 minutes, or until the sauce has thickened. Serve at once with the potato and apple mash and a crisp green salad.

moroccan chicken

PREP TIME: 10 MINUTES +
5 MINUTES STANDING
COOKING TIME: 35 MINUTES
SERVES 4

1 tablespoon Moroccan spice blend (see Note)
800 g (1 lb 12 oz) chicken thigh fillets, trimmed and halved
1 tablespoon oil
3 tablespoons butter
1 large onion, cut into wedges
1 cinnamon stick
2 garlic cloves, crushed
2 tablespoons lemon juice
250 ml (1 cup) chicken stock
75 g ($1/3$ cup) pitted prunes, halved
225 g ($1 1/2$ cups) couscous
lemon wedges, to serve

NUTRITION PER SERVE: Fat 32 g; Carbohydrate 56 g; Protein 46.5 g; Dietary Fibre 3 g; Cholesterol 212.5 mg; 2905 kJ (695 Cal)

1 Sprinkle half the spice blend over the chicken. Heat the oil and 20 g ($1/2$ oz) of the butter in a large saucepan or deep-sided frying pan over medium heat. Cook the chicken in batches for 5 minutes, or until evenly browned. Remove from the pan, then add the onion and cinnamon stick and cook for 2–3 minutes before adding the garlic. Return the chicken to the pan and add the lemon juice and the remaining spice mix. Season to taste, then simmer, covered, for 5 minutes.

2 Add the stock and prunes to the pan and bring to the boil. Reduce the heat to medium–low and cook, uncovered, for 15 minutes, or until the chicken is cooked and the liquid has reduced to a sauce. Before serving, stir 20 g ($1/2$ oz) of the butter into the sauce.

3 About 10 minutes before the chicken is ready, place the couscous in a heatproof bowl, add 375 ml ($1 1/2$ cups) boiling water, and leave for 3–5 minutes. Stir in the remaining butter and fluff with a fork until the butter has melted and the grains separate. Serve with the chicken.

note: Depending on the quality and freshness of the Moroccan spice blend you buy, you may need to use a little more than specified in the recipe.

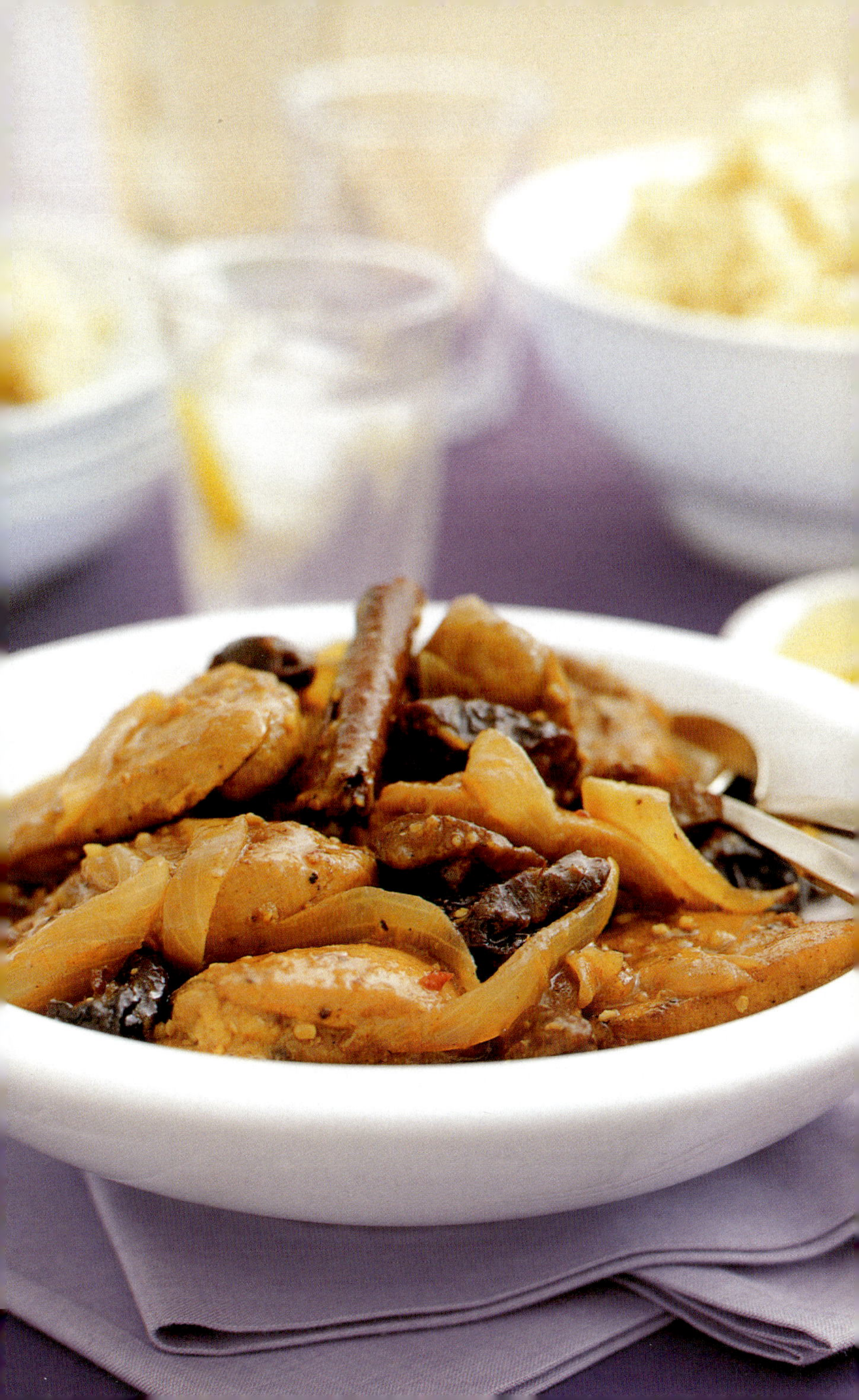

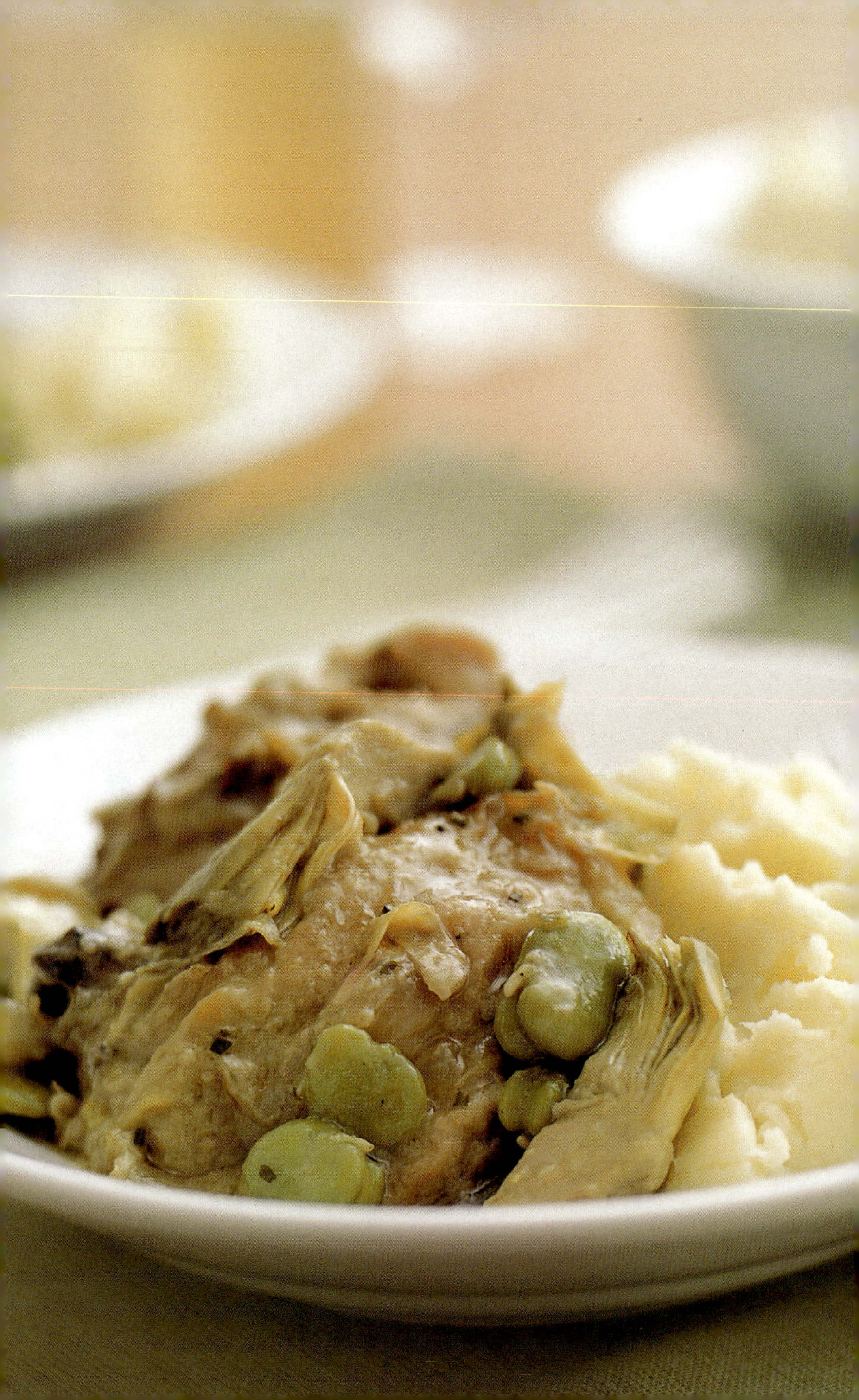

chicken, artichoke and broad bean stew

PREP TIME: 15 MINUTES
COOKING TIME: 1 HOUR 25 MINUTES
SERVES 4

155 g (1 cup) frozen broad (fava) beans
8 chicken thighs on the bone (skin removed, optional)
3 tablespoons seasoned plain (all-purpose) flour
2 tablespoons oil
1 large red onion, cut into small wedges
125 ml (1/2 cup) dry white wine
310 ml (1 1/4 cups) chicken stock
2 teaspoons finely chopped rosemary
350 g (12 oz) marinated artichokes, well drained and quartered
800 g (1 lb 12 oz) potatoes, cut into large cubes
3 tablespoons butter

NUTRITION PER SERVE: Fat 47 g; Carbohydrate 43 g; Protein 75.5 g; Dietary Fibre 8.5 g; Cholesterol 334 mg; 3845 kJ (920 Cal)

1 Remove the skins from the broad beans. Coat the chicken in the flour, shaking off the excess. Heat the oil in a saucepan or flameproof casserole dish over medium heat, then brown the chicken in two batches on all sides. Remove and drain on crumpled paper towels.

2 Add the onion to the pan and cook for 3–4 minutes, or until soft but not brown. Increase the heat to high, pour in the wine and boil for 2 minutes, or until reduced to a syrup. Stir in 250 ml (1 cup) of the stock and bring just to the boil, then return the chicken to the pan with the rosemary. Reduce the heat to low and simmer, covered, for 45 minutes.

3 Add the artichokes to the pan, increase the heat to high and return to the boil. Reduce to a simmer and cook, uncovered, for 10–15 minutes. Add the beans and cook for a further 5 minutes.

4 Meanwhile, cook the potato in a large saucepan of boiling water for 15–20 minutes, or until tender. Drain, then return to the pan. Add the butter and the remaining stock and mash with a potato masher. Serve on the side of the stew.

roast lemon chicken with baked vegetables

PREP TIME: 15 MINUTES +
 10 MINUTES STANDING
COOKING TIME: 1 HOUR 20 MINUTES
SERVES 4

1.5 kg (3 lb 5 oz) whole chicken
4 tablespoons lemon juice
1/2 lemon
9 garlic cloves, whole and unpeeled
4 tablespoons olive oil
1 kg (2 lb 4 oz) roasting potatoes, cut into 5 cm (2 inch) pieces
4 red onions, cut into quarters
8 small zucchini (courgettes), trimmed and cut in half lengthways
250 ml (1 cup) chicken stock

NUTRITION PER SERVE: Fat 41 g; Carbohydrate 57 g; Protein 45 g; Dietary Fibre 10 g; Cholesterol 160 mg; 3255 kJ (775 Cal)

1 Preheat the oven to 220°C (425°F/Gas 7). Put the chicken in a large roasting tin. Pour 1 tablespoon of the lemon juice over the chicken, then place the lemon half and 1 garlic clove inside the cavity. Brush the outside with 1 tablespoon of the oil. Season.

2 Arrange the potato and remaining garlic cloves around the chicken. Brush the potatoes with 2 tablespoons of the oil and roast for 20 minutes. Reduce the heat to 190°C (375°F/Gas 5). Place the onion around the chicken, turning the potatoes at the same time. Return to the oven for a further 30 minutes.

3 Place the zucchini cut-side-down on a baking tray and brush with the remaining oil, then place in the oven. Baste the chicken with its pan juices and pour the remaining lemon juice over the top. Turn the onion and potatoes and roast for 20 minutes, or until the chicken is golden and the juices run clear when pierced between the breast and thigh.

4 Transfer the chicken, potatoes, garlic and onion to a serving plate, cover with foil and keep warm for 10 minutes. Check the zucchini halves are tender and nicely coloured—they may need to stay in the oven.

5 Meanwhile, to make the gravy, place the roasting tin over high heat and add the chicken stock. Stir with a wooden spoon to scrape up any sediment and boil for 7–8 minutes, or until it reduces and thickens.

6 To serve, remove the lemon and garlic from the cavity and discard. Serve the chicken with the onion, garlic, zucchini, potatoes and gravy.

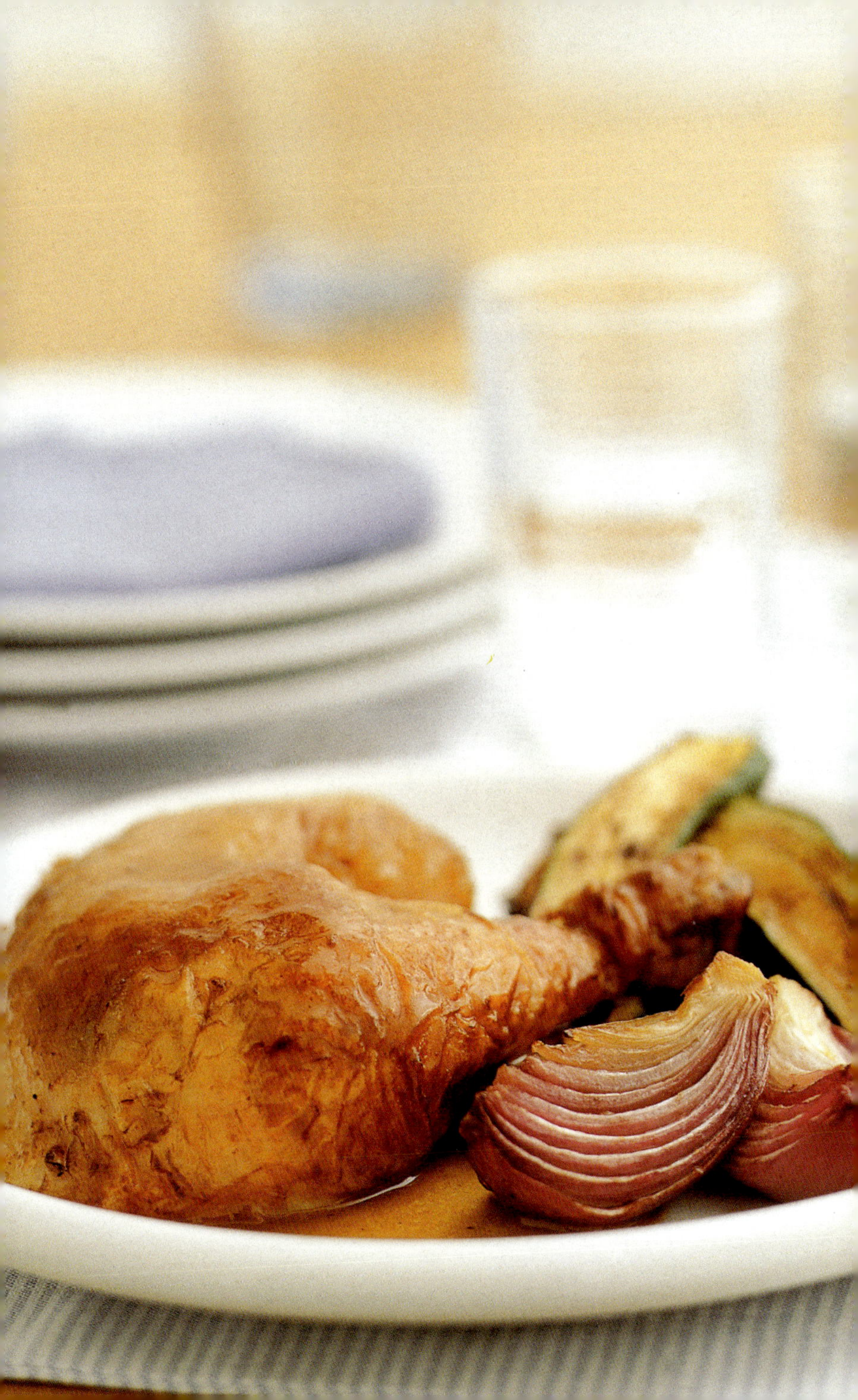

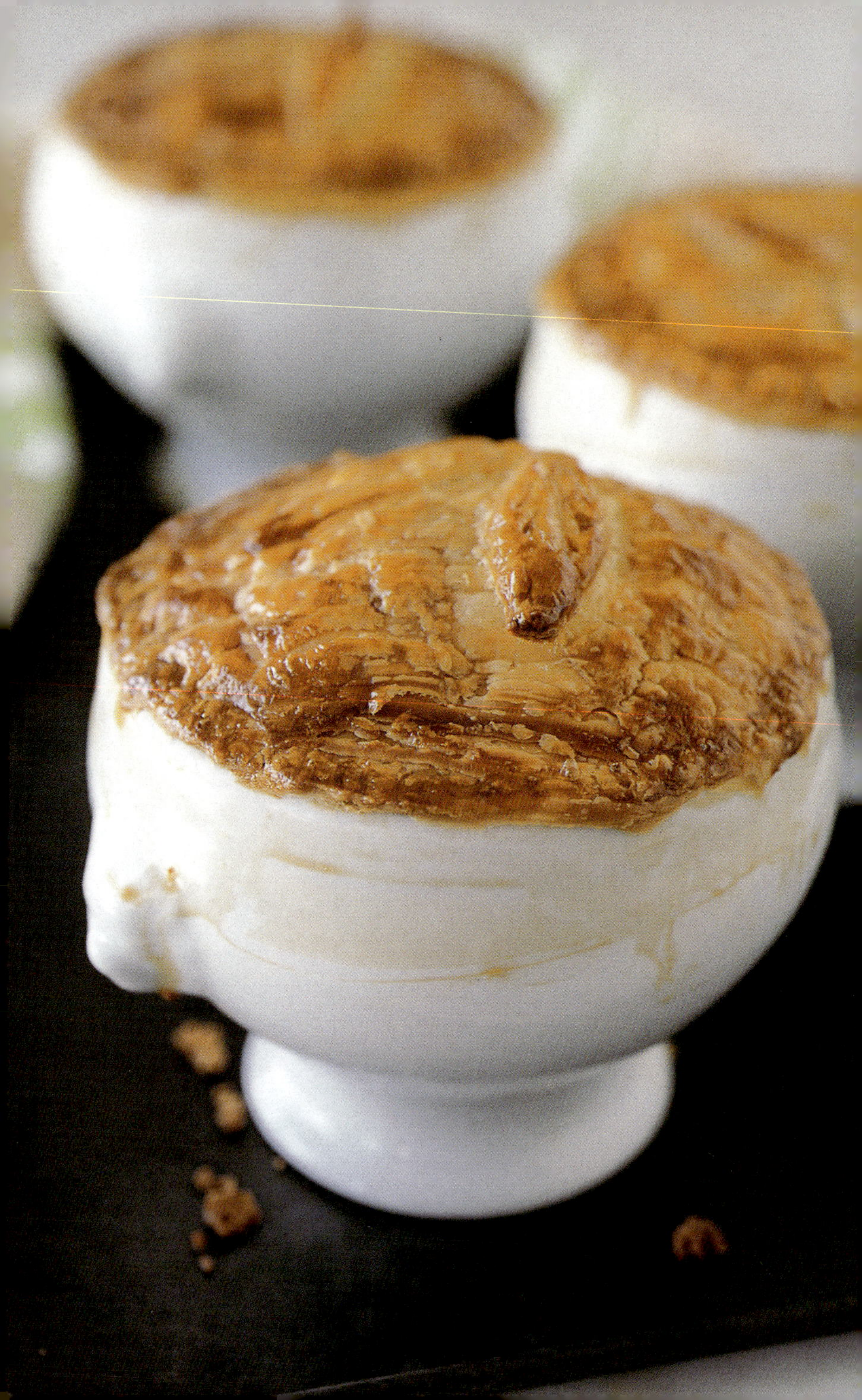

chicken and mushroom pies

PREP TIME: 25 MINUTES
COOKING TIME: 1 HOUR 10 MINUTES
SERVES 4

2 tablespoons olive oil
500 g (1 lb 2 oz) chicken thighs, cut into 2 cm ($3/4$ inch) dice
3 tablespoons butter
1 leek, thinly sliced
3 garlic cloves, crushed
150 g ($5^{1}/2$ oz) Swiss brown mushrooms, sliced
3 tablespoons dry white wine
2 tablespoons plain (all-purpose) flour
250 ml (1 cup) chicken stock
125 ml ($1/2$ cup) cream
2 tablespoons chopped parsley
1 tablespoon finely chopped sage
2 sheets butter puff pastry
1 egg, lightly beaten

NUTRITION PER SERVE: Fat 58.5 g; Carbohydrate 30 g; Protein 32.5 g; Dietary Fibre 3 g; Cholesterol 251.5 mg; 3260 kJ (780 Cal)

1 Heat the olive oil in a heavy-based frying pan and cook the chicken in two batches over high heat for 3–4 minutes each batch, until lightly browned but not cooked all the way through. Remove from the pan with a slotted spoon.

2 Melt the butter in the same pan and cook the leek and garlic over low heat for 6–8 minutes, or until soft. Add the mushrooms and cook for another 6–8 minutes. Return the chicken to the pan. Add the wine and boil for 2–3 minutes, or until nearly all the wine has evaporated. Sprinkle the flour over the top, stir for 1 minute, then add the stock and cream. Reduce the heat and simmer gently for 20 minutes, or until the chicken is tender and the sauce has reduced and thickened. Season to taste, remove from the heat and cool. Stir in the parsley and sage.

3 Preheat the oven to 200°C (400°F/ Gas 6). To make individual pot pies, divide the mixture among four 315 ml ($1^{1}/4$ cup) ramekins. Cut four 12 cm (5 inch) rounds from the pastry, brush the ramekin rims with a little beaten egg, then place the pastry lids on top. Press the rims down firmly to seal. Cut out the pastry scraps and decorate the tops if you wish, brush with egg and cut three steam holes in each pie with a sharp knife. Bake on the bottom shelf for 15–20 minutes, until the pastry is golden.

note: To make one large pie, place the mixture in a shallow 23 cm (9 inch) pie dish, roll the two sheets of pastry together and place over the mixture. Seal the edges with a fork. Make several small steam holes in the pastry with a sharp knife. Brush with beaten egg and bake in a 180°C (350°F/ Gas 4) oven for 30–35 minutes, or until golden.

thai green chicken curry with coriander rice

PREP TIME: 10 MINUTES
COOKING TIME: 20 MINUTES
SERVES 4

250 g (1 1/4 cups) jasmine rice
1 tablespoon vegetable oil
1–2 tablespoons good-quality Thai green curry paste
4 makrut (kaffir) lime leaves (see Note)
1 tablespoon fish sauce
2 teaspoons palm sugar or soft brown sugar
400 ml (14 fl oz) tin coconut cream
750 g (1 lb 10 oz) skinless chicken breast fillets, cut into strips
4 tablespoons roughly chopped coriander (cilantro) leaves
2 tablespoons whole coriander (cilantro) leaves

NUTRITION PER SERVE: Fat 38.5 g; Carbohydrate 56 g; Protein 47 g; Dietary Fibre 3.5 g; Cholesterol 124 mg; 3170 kJ (760 Cal)

1 Bring a large saucepan of water to the boil. Add the rice and cook for 12 minutes. Drain well.

2 Meanwhile, heat the oil over high heat in a wok, then add the curry paste and lime leaves and fry over medium–high heat for 1–2 minutes, or until fragrant. Add the fish sauce and palm sugar and mix well. Pour in the coconut cream, bring to the boil, and then add the chicken strips. Reduce the heat to medium and simmer for 12–15 minutes, or until the sauce is reduced and the chicken is tender and cooked through.

3 Just before serving, stir the chopped coriander through the rice. Serve the curry over the coriander rice, garnished with a few whole coriander leaves.

note: Kaffir lime leaves are shiny, dark and fragrant. Each leaf is shaped in a figure of eight—in our recipes, half of the eight represents one leaf.

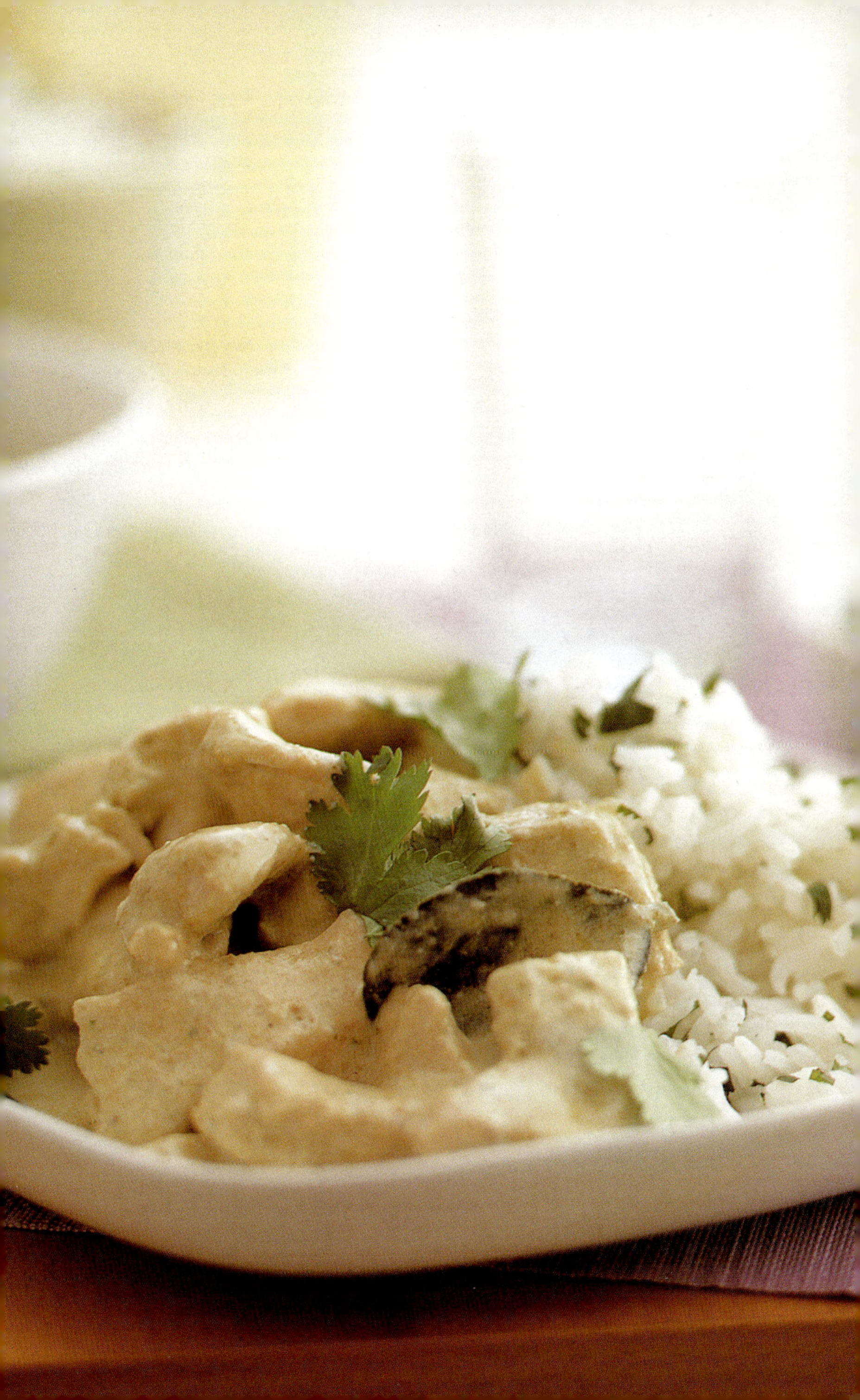

index

apple and potato mash, Chicken and cider stew with, 53
artichoke and broad bean stew, Chicken, 57

baked vegetables, Roast lemon chicken with, 58
butter chicken, Indian, 37

chargrilled chicken, Lime and coriander, 22
Chicken and cider stew with apple and potato mash, 53
Chicken and corn soup, 9
Chicken and mushroom pies, 61
Chicken and mushroom pilau, 45
Chicken and vegetable soup, 5
Chicken and vegetable stir-fry, 25
Chicken, artichoke and broad bean stew, 57
Chicken breast stuffed with tomato, goat's cheese and asparagus, 46
Chicken cacciatora, 29
Chicken, mango and walnut salad, 13
Chicken noodle soup, 5
Chicken stock, 2
Chicken tagine, 34
Chicken waldorf salad, 13
chilli caramel sauce, Stir-fried chicken with, 26
Coq au vin, 33
Cream of chicken soup, 6
Creamy chicken with tarragon and mustard, 30
curry with coriander rice, Thai green chicken, 62

Honey chicken, 42

Indian butter chicken, 37

Lime and coriander chargrilled chicken, 22

Moroccan chicken, 54
mushroom pies, Chicken and, 61
mushroom pilau, Chicken and, 45

Parmesan chicken with quick salsa verde, 50
pies, Chicken and mushroom, 61

roast chicken, Spicy, 49
Roast lemon chicken with baked vegetables, 58

Salad
  Chicken, mango and walnut salad, 13
  Chicken waldorf salad, 13
  Vietnamese poached chicken salad, 10
Salt and pepper chicken with Asian greens and oyster sauce, 49
Satay chicken, 21
Sichuan chicken, 41
Soup
  Chicken and corn soup, 9
  Chicken and vegetable soup, 5
  Chicken noodle soup, 5
  Cream of chicken soup, 6
soy mushroom sauce, Steamed chicken breast with Asian greens and, 38
Spicy roast chicken, 49
Steamed chicken breast with Asian greens and soy mushroom sauce, 38
Steamed chicken with ginger and spring onion sauce, 17
Stir-fried chicken with chilli caramel sauce, 26
stir-fry, Chicken and vegetable, 25
stock, Chicken, 2

Tandoori chicken, 18
tarragon and mustard, Creamy chicken with, 30
Teriyaki chicken with ginger chive rice, 14
Thai green chicken curry with coriander rice, 62

vegetable stir-fry, Chicken and, 25
Vietnamese poached chicken salad, 10